The Murder of John Codman

Richard Lindstrom, PhD.

ISBN-13: **978-1981670505**
ISBN-10: **1981670505**

A Note to the Reader

The story you are about to read is true. It is a story that is frightening and filled with heartbreak. While these events occurred more than 250 years ago, they still have an impact on us today. Since before our country began, we have always struggled for our freedoms. Throughout our history some of us have been less involved than others, and some of us have done more than others for the freedoms we love. We have always had strong views about freedom. All of us have benefited from the sacrifices of others – who have gone before us and those who are impacting our freedoms today. Not much has been written about the story you are going to read. It is, however, an important piece of our history. In the pages to come, you will learn about a terrible tragedy that also proves a valuable lesson in the real cost of freedom during a complex time in America and the world.

Acknowledgements

Thanks to my wonderful wife Carmen
who has been very patient with me for over three
years on this project.

Many thanks to CI Writing Services for outstanding
research, development, expansion, structural
guidance, planning, and publication.

Thanks to Betty Huth and Ed Booth for the
cover design and development.

Thanks to a number of readers for their insight
especially Lisa Jordan for her proof reading.

Thanks to the Codman Estate and the Mayflower
Registry for their Genealogy assistance.

Thanks to The Massachusetts Historic society, The
Paul Revere House, and the
New England Historic Society for their help.

Special thanks to the late Ester Forbes (1891-
1967) who's skillful and comprehensive work on
Paul Revere led me to this story and inspired me to
write this book.

Table of Contents

Cast of Characters

Captain John Codman - A Sea Captain who is also a wealthy Boston land owner and a member of the elite Brahmin upper class, the highest-ranking class in Boston. The Codman family lives in Boston and rents a home from Dr. Clark, even though they own a large 16-acre farm in Lincoln just outside Boston which they purchased in 1740.

John Codman II – the son and heir of Captain Codman

John Codman III – son of John Codman II (age 5 months)

Mark Codman - slave of Captain Codman

Phillis Codman - wife of Mark and slave of Captain Codman

Phoebe Codman - slave of Captain Codman and wife of Quaco

Mr. Salmon - slave owner, thought to have been murdered by poison in 1751 by his slaves, the murder went undetected by the authorities

Kerr - slave of Dr. John Gibbons, from whom Mark requested Arsenic poison, he refused

Dr. William Clark - doctor and landowner, who rented to many Captains of Boston

Robin - slave of Dr. Clark, from whom Mark and Phoebe requested poison to be taken from the doctor's apothecary stores

Thomas Powers - slave owner

Essex - slave of Powers, who provided Mark with Black lead to mix with the Arsenic powder

Quaco - slave of James Dalton and husband of Phoebe

James Dalton - slave owner and Quaco's master

William Stoddard - Justice of the Peace who examined witnesses

Thaddeus Mason - Attorney General

John Remington – Coroner

Sixteen grand jury witnesses – who gave oaths that the coroner statement of Codman's death by poison is true

Caleb Dana - Grand Jury Foreman

Stephen Sewall - Chief Justice

Benjamin Lynde - Associate Justice

John Cushing – Associate Justice

Chambers Russell – Associate Justice
(Note: Chambers Russell purchased the Lincoln Boston estate in 1740. Chambers Russell had no children, but his niece Margaret Russell would eventually marry John Codman III. Their child, Charles Russell Codman, was the heir to the estate hence the name today, Codman estate.)

Also living in Boston in 1755

Samuel Adams - age 33 - Founding father

Benedict Arnold - age 20 - British loyalist and American trader

John Hancock - age 18 - Founding father

Patrick Henry - age 17 - American hero "Give me liberty or give me death"

Joseph Warren - age 10 - American hero

Paul Revere - age 21- American hero

James Otis – American hero "no taxation without representation"

John Adams - age 20 - 2nd US President

Benjamin Franklin had recently moved from Boston to Philadelphia

Chapter 1

The Gaol

Mark Codman's life as a slave had now changed forever. The cell which held him was dark and depressing. The stone walls were thick, at some estimates nearly three and a half feet, with door locks and bolts requiring eight-inch keys. It was a formidable fortress, partitioned into cells with planks and boards, all fortified against escape with unglazed windows barred with iron. The sweltering heat of this 1755 late summer day enveloped the cell and intensified the stench of human excrement and incessant sweat.

Inside Mark's cell was a filthy meager pillow, and a worn blanket which provided little comfort. In the corner was a bucket for bodily functions which remained unattended for long periods of time. Mark heard the scurrying about of rats on the dirt floor amid the miserable groans of despondent and dejected souls who were committed to this awful jail on Old Prison Lane. This was the Boston Gaol of Queen Street, steps from the new State House. It was suffocating, unbearable, and inescapable. Mark was well aware that no one had ever escaped this prison.

As the clock struck dolefully on the hour, Mark sat alone, chained in his cell, contemplating the sins which led him to this dreadful place. His thoughts ran the gamut, from justification for the suffering he experienced at the hands of his slave master Captain John Codman, to guilt at having taken another man's life.

Mark thought of the long, unending hours he was forced to labor on the docks, loading and unloading his master's merchant ships. He loathed the work and the hours, as well as the disrespect of his master, who after many a long day's work would loan him out to others on a whim, which forced him to be separated from his wife and children for long periods at a time. Of course, worst of all, was the heartless sale of his five-year-old son, by that cold bastard

Codman. It had torn out his heart and nearly broken his family once and for all.

Mark's son, at five, had grown old enough to work in a new owner's home without being an undue burden of care and thus the boy commanded a fair price and would no longer be a financial drain for Codman. In Codman's eyes, Mark and his wife would be more productive without the preoccupation and attachment of the child. The feelings of mother, father, and child were of no consequence to a slave owner like Captain John Codman.

Mark then recalled his hopes and dreams of a kinder master and even the possibility of gaining his freedom – the freedom he longed for, which was now dashed in light of his arrest. Mark's emotions were on a rolling tide, as he contemplated his fate and the fate of those who had aided his efforts to escape the humiliating bonds of slavery in the Codman household, and live his life in peace with what remained of his family.

His ponderings were interrupted by another prisoner, Phillis Codman, his beloved wife, a fellow slave at Codman House and one of Mark's co-conspirators. She spoke softly to Mark, as best she could, though the wooden walls offering words of comfort. "Mark, I love you."

Mark, in turn, attempted to reassure her. "I love you, too, my dove. And I'm so sorry."

"Oh, Mark, don't make an apology. I knew, just like you did, what could happ'n if we were caught. In spite of our dreams of a free life and some happiness."

"Yes, I know lovey, but still, the idea was mine. I couldn't stand it no longer the thought of losing you or our remaining young'uns by Codman's notions and to line his pockets."

"I know, Mark, I know." Phillis sat, silenced now by her own thoughts, lost hopes of a life with a kinder master or even a life of real freedom with Mark and their children. She knew they would never likely know the whereabouts of the son they had lost, but she had hoped maybe they could live a life of peace together, as their own masters.

Yet now, here they sat, imprisoned, wondering aloud at their fate. Having been arrested and accused so quickly after the crime had surprised them.

Mark had often told Phillis and the other slaves the stories he'd heard - tales of slaves who had poisoned their masters and gotten away with it – no prison, no punishment – a happily ever after for the slaves who ended up in considerably better conditions and some even set free.

Mark had dared not mention other stories he'd heard of slaves attempting escape or even murder who were caught and suffered an unspeakable fate. Always fresh in his mind was the legend of Mr. Salmon, a slave owner, who died in 1751, purportedly murdered by poison administered by his slaves. The plot and the slaves involved remained a mystery, undiscovered. Mark had truly believed the legend when he put his plan in motion and that it was entirely justified and even possible to get away with murder. It hadn't been hard to convince Phillis and Phoebe, who were also desperate for freedom, after he told them the stories.

Ironically, it was his master, Captain John Codman, who had taught Mark to read, specifically so he could carry on minor business for the Captain when needed at the docks and read the Bible. And read he had, believing the murder of his cruel master was condoned by the Word, because no blood would be shed to perpetrate the act. Mark had read the Bible passages to Phillis and later to Phoebe, convincing them God was on their side. And so, their plan had proceeded and succeeded, or so they thought until the authorities came for them.

Phoebe Codman was not part of the conversation on this humid, heavy night in the jail. She laid unconscious on the prison floor, beaten senseless by her fellow prisoners for the betrayal of her co-conspirators. Phoebe was instantly labeled a traitor not only for her part in her master's murder, but also, paradoxically, as word of her confession spread throughout the jail. The gaol's guards stood idly by and allowed the beating to occur, only stepping in to save her when she became unconscious. After all, it wouldn't be proper to allow her to die without the public spectacle of a Parade of Death to come, should the death penalty be imposed.

Every slave knew Captain Codman was an important man in Boston, but they were just now beginning to understand the shock and outrage the citizens of Boston felt at his murder. Mark, Phillis, and Phoebe would soon learn that in Boston, morality and social order would only be maintained by the swift and heavy-handed carriage of justice.

Mark, Phillis, and Phoebe's fate would soon join the haunted whispers often heard in the Queen Street Gaol's dark, dank hallways, murmured by the spirits of those whose captive souls had been detained within these same walls. The long, lost voices of "witches" Mary Parsons, Sarah Osborne, and "Goody" Glover cried mournfully, amid the creaking walls and jangling chains, for truth in lieu of execution. The echoing shouts of the famed pirate Captain Kidd, shackled years earlier called for parlay before he was shipped to London to be drawn, hanged, and quartered for treason. The words of freedom, penned by newspaper men James Franklin and Daniel Fowle, seemed to echo the sentiments of Mark, Phillis, and Phoebe's dashed dreams in the haunted whispers of the gaol.

Prisoners did not linger long in these cell walls, as trials and sentencing were carried out swiftly under British Colonial Law. The Massachusetts Bay Colony prisoners accused and convicted of all manner of moral and criminal activity were housed together in the plain 60 by 40-foot Boston building complete with a dungeon and whipping post, fitted with chains and manned with floggers. At any given time, the prison might house Quakers objecting to Puritan rules, rebels against the Crown, debtors, slaves, indentured servants, pirates, Indians, witches, and even editors and writers who released propaganda against British rule and cried out for freedom.

In the prison this day, Mark, Phoebe, and Phillis, were those charged with the most heinous crime - murder. But also, held in the gaol was a gentleman called John, who had been heard swearing in the street at his wife and promptly arrested. Mr. and Mrs. James Chilton were present as well, having failed to attend the last church service; their excuse didn't matter.

A Mr. Eaton was imprisoned for speaking, seemingly in the shadows, to Miss Minter, considered by all in Boston as an inappropriate action toward the opposite sex. A man named Thomas and a man called Ely also shared the prison spaces, caught drunk and brawling in the streets; from the sound of it they continued to carry on, something that would not help their cause.

Mark knew confessions were often forced using scribes to pen the falsified admissions of guilt. Prisoners were often shackled, chained to the walls, floors, or one another, and flogged at the whipping post to compel compliance. Mark knew well that this tactic was commonly used for tough lessons not meant for public consumption. Unlike the wealthy, who could often see their sentence waived or reduced with the paying of fines to the authorities – for murder by a slave there would be little chance of reprieve.

And yet for Mark and Phillis, the gaol did not exist as punishment itself, but was only the holding area for the penalty to come. Most punishment existed in the way of fines, time in the stockades, public confessions intended to shame the convicted into better behavior, the dunking stool, branding with a hot iron, often used for adulterers, drunkenness, blasphemy or slander, rogues, thieves, and those convicted of manslaughter, as well as flogging, banishment, and worst of all, death by hanging.

Mark, Phillis, and Phoebe knew these sentences were carried out as public events, which often drew crowds of thousands to view the Parade of Death. They had been witness to such events – led by ministers, city officials, and the prisoner, whose repentant cries for mercy could be heard even over the din of the frenzied crowds. These public displays gave the ministers and city officials a spellbound audience whom they could encourage to lead a virtuous lifestyle while condemning the evil behaviors and crimes which come from the influence of Satan and his demons.

They had all seen the vilest public spectacles for the most horrifying crimes which terminated with the execution of the convicted prisoner. Often the dead bodies of these prisoners were displayed for days, weeks, or longer as an ominous warning to the citizenry of the penalty for such treacherous acts.

Mark and Phillis were each suspended in their own thoughts, as they were returned to the grim reality of their situation by the dejected voices of others accused of lesser crimes, who lingered in cells beside them.

Mark contemplated the stark difference of the prison cell from what he now saw as the comforts of the Codman Estate. Here, in the gaol, there was no place to wash, no privacy at all. They were hungry. They struggled to hold onto hope with prayer. The food on which they now subsisted was gruel, a watery, mealy mixture of potatoes, oats, and onions, salt, and pepper and on rare occasions some sort of meat. The gruel was accompanied by bread and water all in definitive contrast to the meals Phillis had prepared for them at Codman House – fish, chicken, pork, beef, and possum, along with beans, cabbage, collards, corn, onions, peas, potatoes, and pumpkins.

Memories flooded Mark's mind. His thoughts ran to and fro until Phillis, dread overwhelming her, interrupted his thoughts with a question. "What you think will happen to us, Mark? And what about our wee ones?"

Mark, in an effort to reassure her, replied, "Maybe we'll be needed elsewhere, and be allowed back to work with supervision. Then we can keep caring for our babes, too." Even as the words escaped his mouth, he knew it would not be so. They were slaves, without rights, who had been accused of the murder of their master. Their remaining children would be raised by someone else, or sold to other slavers. Mark knew their future would not be bright. From her silence, he knew Phillis knew it as well.

They had been in prison only days, but dread had overcome them. The arrest stated Petit Treason, a crime that Mark, Phillis, nor Phoebe knew was considered crueler and wickeder than murder alone, for it bore the element of betrayal and intensified the nature of the crime. The punishment would have to send a message to the slaves of Boston and beyond.

It would not be long before the trial, and the conspirators would discover their fate. In fact, if convicted, their sentence would be carried out swift and sure - as early as

the following morning. There would be no appeal

forthcoming and certainly no one would dare challenge the

sentences of slaves who had murdered their master.

Chapter 2

The City

The morning of 1 July 1755 dawned bright and beautiful, a calm late summer day. Walking along Pinkney Street, were George a Negro freeman, Prince a mixed-race freeman, James a British citizen, and John a white citizen of Boston, discuss the recent events.

Edward, a white slave holder, seeing his friend John, crosses the street to greet him. As he approaches the men, he wished he had remained where he was, going about his business on the other side of the street. Though he counts John as a good friend, he knows John's opinions often go against the fundamental colonial ideals, particularly in regard to slavery. He cannot turn back now, as John has seen him and offers a greeting.

"Good morrow, Edward. I believe you know these gentlemen."

"Why yes, good morning all." Edward focuses his eyes on John and James, finally glancing somewhat uncomfortably at George and Prince.

"Edward, we were just discussing the Codman murder." John offered, turning his attention back to George, "Carry on then, George."

"Slavery lead to this spectacle. Mark and Phillis Codman would likely not be in the gaol facing death today had they not yearned for freedom so fervently," George spoke, looking directly at Edward.

Prince nodded in agreement, "Captain Codman would also be alive, and his house not in mourning. If men were to treat one another with respect and equality, and honor one another the way God intended, slavery would cease to exist."

"Maybe so, Prince, but you fly in the face of society ... Can freedom exist alongside slavery?" James questioned.

"Slavery keeps the factories running and the fields producing, fellows." Edward spoke jokingly at first, but then turned serious, "Would any of you work the fields or toil in the factories to keep the colony going, I wonder? And of course, I have to ask, do you truly believe a slave has the right to murder his master?"

"And I must answer your questions with questions, sir, do you truly believe the prevailing notion that people, like myself, are unable to be educated, intended for all time to be subservient?" George interjected quickly.

"No sir, like yourself, several of my slaves are well-educated."

'Well then, I must respectfully ask, should you offer them the choice of freedom or to continue in slavery in your service today, what would they say?"

"I cannot say, though they seem happy in my service."

"Well, sir, maybe you are a far kinder master than most, certainly far better than is my experience."

"Stop, right there! Though some of your kind are capable of education, others are certainly not and only respond to the firm hand and stern guidance of their superiors. Now if you gentlemen will excuse me, I fear, we will not come to an agreement this day on this subject. God rest Cap'n Codman. And I bid you Good Day, gentlemen!" And with that Edward was gone, back across the street into the bustling crowd.

John debated whether to go after his friend, but instead remained, "Unlike my friend Edward, I believe freedom is a natural right, given us by God, a right that men might try to deny other men. The sad part is these atrocities to which we have been witness are simply a result of the enslavement of men who would be free and the staunch, if incorrect, belief that some men are inferior to others and deserve to be enslaved. If given the choice would not all men prefer freedom to slavery?"

"Absolutely true, and for that matter, wouldn't a free man like any of us, prefer even death over slavery, if given no other choice?" James added completing the thought. With that, the fellows nod in agreement as each goes on his separate way to attend to his duties, lost in thoughts of freedom, slavery, and death.

They were not alone. The tumult of the recent murder and the emotional upheavals had left rampant anger and lingering questions in the air that enveloped Boston and the surrounding countryside. In Harvard Yard, Dr. Benjamin Willard and Justice J.P. Eliot discussed the details of the Codman case in light of the convictions of the citizenry of the greater Boston region.

"J.P., you know that colony firmly holds to the conviction that there exists an upper class, a working class, a lower class, and a criminal class, with the criminal element being under the firm control of Satan," Dr. Willard stated matter of factly.

"Yes, you're right Ben, it is the conventional imperial structure, based on British tradition and heavily influenced by the Puritans," Justice Eliot nodded in agreement.

"When one considers that roughly eight percent of the population of Boston is black, it remains difficult to believe that among the lesser educated masses that the color black is associated with the demonic and evil."

"True, but it is thusly so, it remains Negro slaves are still thought exotic as well as strange and even dangerous."

"Considering that slavery in the colonies is now commonplace, having developed quickly on the heels of the first slaves who arrived in Jamestown, Virginia, almost 150 years ago, one would think the people would have overcome some of their prejudices about blacks and their ability to learn," Willard pondered.

"One would think so, but as the other fledgling colonies follow suit, we stand here in the first of the colonies to legalize slavery over 100 years prior with only one small change. As you are certainly aware, Ben, the early slave laws applied to slaves of any color, Africans, Indians, and even Europeans but was quickly changed to prohibit Blacks and Indians from keeping white servants. And then later came the legislation transforming all imported black servants into slaves for life. So rather than gaining a greater understanding of blacks, the colonists seem to have grown more suspicious." J.P. offered.

"You are absolutely correct, and so it continues, as the oppression grew worse only 50 years past as laws were passed restricting the movement of Negroes, and requiring them to have permission or assignment to go about with any freedom of movement."

"Yes, so true, prior to the passage of that law, blacks were able to live free, own property, possess servants, and marry those of other races. But the times changed. I wonder, is it merely a lack of understanding, my friend? Or is it rather simply oppression built on by fear? Or possibly just punishment intended to legislate morality according to the justice meted out by mortal men?"

Both men, old friends, stood in silence at their thoughts, each preoccupied and meditative, considering the implications and what was to come.

****

In Boston's North End, questions in abundance were also on the lips of a young 12-year-old named Aaron. He was shocked and confused by yesterday's arrests and seeking answers from his father, a former indentured servant, who has risen to the rank of skilled tradesman known for his honesty and hard work. "Papa, why would these slaves kill their master? Don't they know that murder is wrong?"

His father, Francis, hesitatingly answers, "Aaron, we don't yet know what happened to the Cap'n. We'll have to wait for the trial."

"But everyone says they murdered their master? Do you think they did?"

"Son, I don't know, but I can tell you that some masters can be kind, while others can be cruel. There is no way for us to know what kind of master Cap'n Codman was to his slaves. I can only tell you that being under the control of another man is often hard labor. Even as an indentured servant, and knowin' I would one day be free, it was difficult,

35

sometimes near impossible, to be under the orders of another man constantly. And remember, these slaves had no notion of ever being free – there is no way out of slavery – except escape or death."

Aaron looked carefully at his father, whose eyes had welled up with tears. Even though he knew he shouldn't go on, he felt compelled to ask one more question. "So, you think they could have done it, I mean, killed him? Like he was so horrible, they thought it was their only way out?"

"It's possible son, it's entirely possible."

Francis remained silent for a moment and felt the need to continue to try to explain life's harsh, often confusing realities to his son - how life in the British colony truly was – often an unfair world where nearly everyone found themselves fighting to simply survive. Considering all the challenges they daily faced – the threat of smallpox, Indian raids, out of control piracy, the French and Indian War, Britain's taxation, tariffs, along with the quartering, at will, of British troops – how would his son possibly understand?

Outside of Boston Proper, in the countryside, Hanna, a young slave of 11, awakened from a fitful sleep of nightmares. She dreamed she was ripped from her mama's side and sent into a household where she knew no one. It was a nightmare she had before, but tonight it was more intense, more frightening. She had heard her mama and the others talking about the little children of the slaves who'd been arrested, and it brought her fears back, afresh.

She sought out her mother, Bett, for comfort and answers. "Will we ever be free, Mama?"

Her mama hugged her close, and tried to calm her girl with the words, "As God wills it, sweet Hanna." While in her mind and heart, Bett, too, was haunted by the images of murder, the abandoned children, and the seemingly impossible dream of freedom.

****

At Codman house, disarray was the order of the day, as a somber mood enveloped the house. Had their own slaves really turned on them? It truly seemed so. Who, of the remaining slaves could be trusted? After all Mark and Phillis were certainly greatly trusted of all the slaves they owned. And if they had done what they were accused of, would justice prevail? Would punishment be meted out? Would peace come again to their home?

****

In the churches and public buildings, clergymen and city officials alike congratulated themselves on their successful prayers for the capture of the murderers of their friend Captain Codman. They were pleased with their well-organized efforts in promoting moral living among the many citizens of Boston.

Even so, there were others, who would sooner, rather than later become the voices of freedom for all men, who questioned, "Would justice indeed be carried out? Was slavery and the greed that perpetuated the ideal wrong both Biblically and morally? As slavery grew, so would the voices of the young abolitionist movement.

All across Boston, thoughts wandered and questioned yesterday's events. The thoughts and questions as numerous as the citizens of the burgeoning city. Many would view the spectacle to come freely, but the slaves and indentured servants would be compelled by force, if necessary, to watch the events unfold.

Two members of the Boston Board of Selectmen, Mr. Eaton and Mr. Hill, like most in the city that day, found themselves pondering the historical foundations of Boston and their impact on the events of the present.

"We must remain true to our founding in 1630 by Puritans, their values on which our great city stands. When these "original" colonists arrived, they discovered the

Algonquin Indians among the 40 tribes who inhabited what is now known as New England. Joining with these true founders of Massachusetts, the Puritans adopted the Algonquin name "Massa" (large) "Adchu" (hill) "et" (at) – "Massachusetts" (at or about the great hill), calling the area the Massachusetts Bay Colony," Mr. Eaton, a descendant of those early Puritans, boasted.

"I know, Mr. Eaton, but you must also give credit to the citizenry of Boston, which has grown up the area rapidly. The city's excellent harbor made for a powerful fishing industry but also drew a booming slave trade, as well as other commercial endeavors, and also a diverse variety of settlers, which all pour into the city's coffers," Mr. Hill intoned.

"Yes, it's true the streets are a growing mass of narrowly twisted dirt roads, like Philadelphia and other successful cities. And while on these same streets one might see traffic jams of carriages, carts, horse riders, pedestrians, and even livestock, our Puritan values must remain the guiding force. And murder under any circumstances, even slavery, is not an acceptable course of action."

Like all Bostonians, Mr. Hill and Mr. Eaton were proud of their town hall government which afforded them a good measure of self-rule. Yet and still, social order had to be maintained, a fact to which the Codman murder attested to heartily. This, too, seemed a foreshadowing of what Boston would become in the years ahead.

The citizenry of Boston was as diverse as the opinions held regarding the arrests. The Codman family remained – children, John II, Stephen, Richard, Elizabeth, Mary, Benjamin, Ann, Katherine, Isaac, and Parnell, as well as their families, still in mourning, for their own Captain John Codman, head of the household, father, and grandfather. He led the family with a firm hand, this sea captain who became a wealthy Boston land owner and primed his family's rise amid the Boston Brahmin – the wealthy, the influential, the rule makers, the highest-ranking class in Boston.

Codman, himself, fought his way to the top, orphaned at a young age, he had grown up as a ward of Charles Chambers, whose influence likely aided Codman's rise to the ranks among the Boston gentry. Prior to his murder, he found himself entrenched in the upper class, the Harvard educated, those powerful influencers who set the tone of American government and culture, Boston's untitled aristocrats and slave owners one and all.

Though they owned a large farm in Lincoln, the family resided in Boston, in the home they rented from Dr. William Clark. Dr. Clark, in addition to his rank as doctor, was a wealthy landowner himself, owner of the large, bustling Clark wharf and a number of homes in Boston, many of which he rented to other ranking captains. The good doctor was a slaveholder as well, and it just happened that his slave, Robin, worked in keeping the doctor's apothecary storehouse.

Dr. Clark and Captain Codman were representative of the aristocrats of Boston, those who are wealthy, well-educated, and have the all-important right to vote and hold public office. In this ruling class stands the prominent clergy, the magistrates, the landholders, the university professors, high-ranking military officers, and other wealthy professionals. They were the Boston Elite.

Dr. Clark was deeply saddened by the loss of his friend, John Codman. His house slaves recognized it clearly and stepped lightly as they went about their duties on this melancholy day. In the kitchen in whispered tones, house slaves, Meriday and Tandey discussed the control of their master, a well-known member of the Boston Brahmin.

Meriday murmured, "Tandey, have you heard anything about Mark and Phillis this morning?

"No, nothin' more, but you know, like I do, we, as slaves, don't have no rights. Don't matter what we think, but only what Doc and his kind think and that fact is we they property," Tandey sighed.

"Well, we know true, we people, deserve rights, ain't no one should be treated like that ole Cap'n treated his servants. In that respect, we some o' the lucky ones, at least Doc is kind."

"Yeah, he is kind, but we still people, we shouldn't need his permission to marry, or even step outside where we live, we ought ta' be free."

Meriday shook her head in agreement, "Yes, you right. We ought to at least be free like the working-class people, being able to own our own land, crops, or even a small shop, free to get an education, get married, run our own lives."

"It ain't gonna happen soon, 'cause those like the Cap'n and Doc, ain't gonna want ta' give up their control and money in their pockets…"

"Meriday, Meriday, I need my tea!" Tandey stopped short as she heard the Doc call and his footsteps coming in the direction of the kitchen.

Chapter 3

The Slaves

The Codman slaves, Mark, Phillis, and Phoebe are among a relatively small group of slaves in the possession of the Codman family. Like all slaves in Boston, as well as across the cities and countryside of the colonies, they have no rights, but are solely at the mercy of their owners. They exist as property, to be bought and sold, or even given away. In many cases, the slaves are an investment for the masters, a source of prestige among their peers. In other cases, they are simply disposable, tossed away when they fail to meet strict expectations or are too old to work.

Just last year Captain Codman had released an old house slaved believed to be 70 years old or more. After years of service to the Codman family, helping to raise the Codman children; the slave, Mary, was unable to work and was summarily sent to the country to live in the woods of Concord with no money, no income, and no means of support. Mary was essentially banished, now considered a burden to her master, she was left to die alone without family or friends. The Codman's were free of her – free of the cost of care which the Colony would enforce upon them if she were released into the city.

Mark, now the oldest of the Codman slaves, was originally brought to Boston after being stolen away from his family in Africa, and having survived the treacherous journey to America. He recalled it with horror even now as he sat in his jail cell pondering his life.

He remembered his sudden, harrowing departure from Africa; surrounded by armed slavers, both black and white, Mark and the other worthy men from his village had been taken, put into cages on the docks and held against their wills, as the slave ship was made ready. Chained together, he and the others, ripped away from families all over West

Africa, were prodded onto the ship, forced below deck, chained and shackled.

Where were they being taken? Fear overcame many, others hoped to survive. Held in place by their chains in a tiny six-foot space, fed and watered once daily, like livestock, they struggled to breath in the warm, fetid air. Mark saw many die during the passage, some purposefully. They were the troublemakers made examples of to keep the other slaves in check. Others died from heartbreak, and still others from lack of humane conditions on board. The dead were dragged above deck and heaved overboard without a prayer or condolence.

A slave who died on the voyage was merely a calculated loss – the cost of doing business – like product spoilage which is tossed away. Too many dead slaves and there would be little profit as well as hell to pay, making the ship's captain take care not to lose many. Mark lost track of the length of the journey, as days turned into weeks and then months.

When Mark felt he could bear it no more, they arrived. Now came the off-loading in Boston Harbor. Humiliated yet again, they were roughly washed and fed a meager meal. Next, grease was applied to enhance their body's appearance and improve their presentation at the sale. It seemed their appearance as healthy as opposed to the deplorable condition they were in would bring a bigger price to the slave traders. To top off the disgrace, they were then branded as slaves – an 'S' on the arm or leg - applied with a white-hot blacksmith's branding iron. It was a mark that could never be removed, even if they should regain their freedom. Then, the bidding began.

Though Mark had only picked up a few words and common phrases of the words being spoken this day, the intention of his captors, as well as those in the growing crowd of bidders, was clear to him.

"Buying men, women, and children? How could it be?" Mark thought as the auction began and he saw the gleam and greed in the eyes of the men set on making purchases.

Held in what appeared to be a cattle pen, Mark watched as one by one, the would-be slaves were taken from the pen and put on display on the platform. They were forced to open their mouths as buyers prodded and poked. He watched whole families torn apart and sold separately, their degradation and fears complete. They were auctioned, alongside the slightly more fortunate indentured servants, newly arrived from Ireland and England, as well as cattle and furniture.

"Would the humiliation never end?" Mark wondered wearily as he was led to the platform.

As if in a nightmare, he could still hear the auctioneer begin the bidding, "£10."

"£10," rang out a voice in the audience.

"£25," came another bid.

"£40," shouted a third bidder.

"£75."

"£100," and so it continued until finally he heard, "Sold to Cap'n John Codman of Charlestown for £225," the auctioneer concluded his sale.

Mark's dreadful experience would be repeated in some fashion for more than 400 thousand slaves brought to the North America Colonies and more than four million times for the slaves brought to Central and South America.

Mark dared a glance at the man who now "owned" him. "Captain Codman," Mark pondered, "Was that a victorious smile or a revolting smirk?" Mark could not tell if this new master, with a wife on his arm, and children in tow, would be cruel or kind, but he would soon find out.

Mark recalled the pain of seeing this man, the Captain, with his children and waves of despair poured over him. Ever creeping into his mind was the family he lost when he was captured and spirited away to North America. He held back the tears, "How did they fare in his absence? Did they despair as he did? Did they long to be reunited with him or were they, too, captured and sold into slavery in his absence?"

He had to be strong, and in that moment, he realized he would never know.

Now in his cell, he thought of his first family lost, and now it seemed he would lose his second family, as well as whatever happiness he had found.

He recalled how his will to survive aided him in the days that followed. He found his place among the Codman slaves serving the family in a variety of ways. He was strong in spite of his maltreatment aboard the slave ship and in addition, he was a fast learner, though he knew only a few words of English, picked up onboard the ship.

As was the custom (mandatory it was) in the area, encouraged by the Reverend Cotton Mather, he found himself a part of the slave section in the Charlestown Meeting House, learning English and being instructed in the Puritan religion of the Massachusetts Bay Colony.

Incredible as it seemed and much to his surprise, he found himself baptized into this unusual religion of which he had developed a strange, unexplainable fascination. Mark also heard much of the controversy of teaching slaves to read. Many felt teaching slaves to read would make them unmanageable – discontent, unhappy, and distracted by their plight. Others felt if would make the slaves of lesser value to their masters. Others, still, felt that it was a futile effort, not believing slaves had the capacity to learn the art of reading.

Coming to the realization he would never likely return to his African family, Mark had eventually fallen in love, not on purpose, but when it had happened he worked to forge a life with a slave woman who also found herself in service to the Codmans. Mark's eyes filled again with tears as he thought of Phillis, held in a cell nearby, losing everything she held dear by following his leading.

Phillis, in the next cell, was also recalling the life that was now slipping from her grasp. She remembered being ripped from her mother as a little girl and sold to Captain Codman and his family.

Grieved by the loss of her mother, Phillis had miraculously survived her journey on the Boston slave ship, the *Phillis*, a testament to the human spirit. Her beautiful African name, she would never hear again, was discarded and replaced with the name of the ship on which she was transported. Like other slaves, she was also assigned the surname of her master. Phillis was a house servant to the Codman family - Captain John, his wife, Parnell, and their 10 children. Grown into a woman, she had been educated by Parnell Codman in order to help with the large Codman brood.

Phillis met Mark when he was bought to serve the Codmans. They fast became friends, as she was instructed to help him learn the language and teach him to read and write. She saw something in him, maybe it was his sadness due to all he had lost, or maybe it was his determination in spite of it, nonetheless, she wanted to help him endure his enslaved state.

It was difficult at first, Mark was torn between defiance to his new master and his will to survive. She understood exactly how he felt, as they shared similar stories of being torn from the ones they loved.

She remembered those early days with Mark, days when the Cap'n had been a better master, growing his family and his fortune with his wife and children by his side. Mark had eventually settled in and accepted her overtures of help and friendship. Then something changed in his demeanor as he dropped his defiance toward her and seemed to be making an effort to win her respect. At first, she didn't know what to make of it, as he brought her little bouquets and said they were a thank-you for her help and friendship.

She smiled as she remembered his ultimate declaration of love for her, her own surprise, and then the realization that their friendship had grown into something more. The Cap'n had agreed to their marriage at the urging of his wife Parnell. Phillis recollected clearly the argument between the Cap'n and his wife over it, and it became the one and only time he had permitted such a union among his slaves, feeling it created unnecessary distractions for his property – the slaves.

Phillis remembered that day, as if it were yesterday, it was a day when she was happy. Mistress Parnell had presented her with a pale blue handkerchief and a sweet bouquet of posies as Phillis and Mark were married behind the house on the estate. And now, she and her beloved Mark were likely about to leave this life together, their children lost to them forever.

In the next cell, Mark's thoughts turned to his other co-conspirator, Phoebe. In Charlestown, Mark met Phoebe as well, who had fallen in love with a slave called Quaco, who belonged to another slave owner, James Dalton. Mark thought Phoebe's situation was even sadder than his own, she had no recollection of her past, having come to the Codman's early on and now she was wed to a man with whom she could only spend one night a week, when given permission by their masters.

Mark knew as difficult as it had been, that he and Phillis at least enjoyed some semblance of normal married life. Cap'n Codman had reluctantly given his permission for their marriage and children soon became a part of their family. It may have been the only time, outside of his education, that the Cap'n had done a kind deed to Mark.

Mark and Phillis had felt that given their current situation, they at least had each other and their family. But the dream of freedom loomed large in their hearts and minds. Fear often interrupted their dreams as both Mark and Phillis were well aware that their marriage and family could be torn apart at Captain Codman's will and so it had, when the Cap'n so ruthlessly tore away their eldest child from them and sold him without so much as a second thought. His wife no longer there to temper him, the Cap'n had changed drastically for the worst.

Despite many slaves' efforts to form families and forge connections, as property they could be bought and sold by their masters as if they were cattle or farm equipment. No thought was given to the pain caused when a family was separated, divvied up like prize winnings among the slave holders. It was common for babies to be snatched from their mother's arms in infancy and passed along to other households near and far. Mothers and Fathers, alike, left to mourn yet another loss in this life of bondage and oppression in which they found themselves.

Mark, in his recollection, thought that for some time, all went well. Captain Codman permitted Mark to live in Boston with his wife and young children under the proviso that he hire himself out and give his wages to Codman.

It was an arrangement brought on, in part, by Mark's first attempt to get himself sold to a gentler master or freed altogether. Mark believed, because he knew other slaves had done it successfully, if he was nuisance enough, Codman would at best, free him, and at worse, sell him to, hopefully, a kinder master. Though he knew he would never be reunited with his first family, as a freeman he could at least have a life with his new family here in America.

In the end, Mark's plan failed. The only reward was Codman's resulting suspicions. Something in his gut told him that his slaves had been the cause of his losses – but he had no proof, no evidence that tied them to it. Yet his misgivings forced him to make changes, allowing Mark to live in town nearer his wife and children.

In 1752, when Captain Codman's wife, Parnell, had passed away, so did the Captain's self-restraint and all manner of temperance. She had been by his side for many years and borne him 11 children, 10 of whom survived. She had brought the calm and composure to him and now she was gone.

Much to the surprise of the eligible women of the region, Captain Codman, considered quite the catch, showed no intention of taking a new bride. In lieu of a new wife, the Captain gave over the management of the Charlestown household to his eldest daughters, Elizabeth and Mary.

Captain John's loss seemed, to his slaves, to give him over to a mixture of melancholy and wrath. The slaves had all heard his story: orphaned by his parents at only eight years old, followed by the loss of his brother five years hence. After his wife's death, the feelings of sorrow, separation, loss, and desperation (the same emotions his slaves knew all too well) began to manifest outwardly as annoyance, anger, and rage.

The Captain's slave, Tom had been the first to feel the pain of Captain's loss. Tom, not acting as quickly or as correctly as Codman would have liked, was struck in the back by the Captain with the small cow's whip which the Cap'n kept at his side. This blow was followed by a blow to the face, applied by the butt of the whip with such fury that Tom's eye was severely injured, never to fully recover. Tom's subsequent recovery took its toll on the other field hands, who had to take on Tom's duties, as well as on Tom, who, though physically able to work, could no longer perform as he had previously.

It was a common quandary for slaves and their owners. Absolute power corrupts, and absolute power is the legal right of a slave owner in regard to his slaves. The owner's rights were spelled out in the slave codes of the colony along with the status (not rights) of the slaves. The owner could essentially do anything he felt compelled to do to control his slaves. Any man could become a tyrant when the law of absolute power was on his side. Tom and Mark knew that fact intimately, having been party to it and having witnessed its expression among their friends – living and dead.

Mark's manageable and somewhat happy life living and working in Boston came to an end soon after, when in February of 1755, Boston City Officials warned Mark out of the city unless he was supervised full-time. Captain Codman, as his master, called Mark immediately back to the Charlestown estate, tearing him once again from his family. For Mark, it stirred up old memories – separation, loss, desperation, anger, and fear. To make matters worse, without warning, Codman sold Mark's oldest son, aged five. No explanation was required, and none was offered. No information of his son's whereabouts was provided.

In Mark's mind, it was more than he could bear, he could offer no comfort to Phillis either, and though their love was deep and abiding, it was sorely tested at the loss of their firstborn child. The Captain's dastardly behavior, no longer compelled to some measure of kindness by his wife, was becoming worse. First the attack on Mark's friend Tom, and now on his family, and his firstborn. Mark was enraged, first that he had not been able to protect those he loved and cared about and second, the situation showed no signs of improvement - ever. Incensed, the recent episodes brought to rise a foul new focus – one that meant freedom at any cost – REVENGE!

Chapter 4

The Conspiracy

Mark could bear it no more; it was the proverbial straw that broke the camel's back. Years of cruel treatment, demeaning disrespect, and now this second separation from his latest family. First stolen from his homeland and his family at the hands of those of his own race, and then his subsequent sale at the hands of white slave traders and his purchase by white slave holders. And now this, torn apart from his family followed by the sale of his dear son.

Mark learned early on that reuniting with his beloved first family was a goal with little hope and so he had worked to overcome his loss and start a new family in this foreign land. He had succeeded, but little did he know the pain he would bear at the hands of his owner. The hours were long and difficult, loaned out everywhere to work for other men, whose hands were often heavier than his own master.

Regarding his cherished second family here in the colony, Mark at first believed they might be safe from separation. He soon discovered how wrong he could be. Colonial law dictated that slave owners post bond on slaves they freed. Why would any slave owner do that?

He could run, but if he ran there would be the slave hunters chasing him like deer with the dogs. These men made their living catching runaway slaves and bringing them home dead or alive. In many cases, the pay was the same either way. Most importantly, what of his family? Running defeated his deep-seated desire to be with his family, to love and cherish them.

That left only one alternative, after all, *"how much could one man be expected to bear?"* he thought. *I've had enough slaving for Cap'n Codman. I got to get out of here. No more waiting."*

He hatched his plan in that moment of grief and anger. Cap'n Codman needed to be gone, out of the picture completely, then he could be sold to a kinder master or maybe even achieve his greatest dream – maybe he would be free. Mark knew the Cap'n would never sell him, but his heirs might. The Cap'n had been offered £400 for him once, which he had quickly and firmly refused. He believed Mark too valuable an asset.

Mark believed forcing his sale to a kinder master would permit him to see his family more often. Mark had tried once before to force Codman to free him and his other slaves or, at least, sell them to another master. He remembered the time as if it were only yesterday – though it had now been six years.

Mark was the engineer of the plan then, too. Mark convinced his wife, Phillis, their fellow slave, Phoebe, and a couple of the field hands that if they burned the Cap'n's property, he'd be forced to sell them at least and maybe even free them. It had happened before – they'd all heard the stories of slaves who damaged property unbeknownst to their masters forcing the owners to sell their slaves to make up the loss and rebuild the property.

Phillis and Phoebe joined Mark's property destruction plot driven by the anguish of family separation. Mark and Phillis never knew when they would be together, splitting their time between Charlestown and Boston, as well as Mark's loaned-out work which took him from the locations where his wife was assigned. Phoebe's husband, Quaco, was owned by another estate, that of James Dalton, and they could only be together the one night a week when slaves were permitted to gather and visit one another.

The plan was simple and came together hastily. Mark situated the tinder alongside the Blacksmith Shop and Warehouse on the Codman grounds. Later, so as not to arouse suspicion, Phillis went about gathering the shavings. As she walked about the property, a young field slave, Toby, approached, "Whacha doin' over here Miss Phillis?"

"Not that's it's your business, boy, but I'm gathering shavings to stoke up the kitchen ovens." Phillis shut the boy down quickly and went about her business.

While she was out, Phoebe ran to answer when Miss Elizabeth called for Phillis.

"Where is Phillis, Phoebe?" Elizabeth groaned, knowing no one could match the efficiency of Phillis in the task at hand.

"She's out gathering a few things for dinner, Mistress, Can I help?"

"No," came the terse reply, "Send Phillis directly to me when she returns."

"Yes, ma'am."

As the conversation ended, Phoebe returned to the kitchen, she met Phillis in the doorway, headed back out to prepare tinder, carrying hot coals.

Arriving at the Blacksmith Shop, she quickly tossed the coals on the tinder and shavings there and across the way at the Warehouse. She then scampered back to the kitchen, where Phoebe hurried her to Mistress Elizabeth.

Finding her mistress in the parlor, Phillis entered, Miss Elizabeth, can I help you?"

"Where on earth have you been, Phillis?"

"Ma'am I was just gathering some things we needed for the kitchen. I came to you as soon as I returned."

Phillis was relieved that Miss Elizabeth seemed satisfied with the vague explanation and proceeded to give Phillis her instructions.

Success was theirs or so it seemed as the shop, the warehouse, and other farm buildings burned to the ground. But as the days following the fire passed, they realized, sadly, their plan had failed. There was no chatter regarding the possible sale of any slaves to cover the cost of the fire. The Cap'n began to rebuild. Mark, Phillis, and Phoebe heard whispers the Cap'n thought his slaves were behind the fire. He wondered if a single slave acted alone or if they were all in cahoots to bring about his undoing. The problem was any evidence had burned up with his buildings.

As far as Mark was concerned, a single positive turn came from the fire. Rightly so, he'd risked his life with the planning and execution. Following the rebuild of the lost property, the Cap'n had permitted Mark to live with or near his family. It was a dream come true, but it had only lasted four short years.

And now here he was, miserable once more, angry, and filled with dreams of revenge. Poison was his plan, but he would need some collaborators.

Mark knew all about Mr. Salmon, his murder by poison perpetrated by his slaves and never discovered. Mark also knew well the penalty should he and his accomplices fail and be caught – death. It happened all too often. Bess in Prince George attempted to poison her master Beale, and was caught and hanged, as well as Joe, who succeeded in poisoning his Master, but paid by being hanged and was then displayed in chains for all to see. Punishment came quickly when a slave committed a crime, especially against his or her master. It would be a spectacle designed to strike fear into other slaves should Mark fail.

"I'll be dead, should the scheme not come together, but at least I'll be free." Mark pondered. *"Wasn't the possibility of being free here or on the other side with Jesus worth the risk? I've suffered enough — kidnapped, herded like cattle, sold, held as a prisoner and forced to labor at the whims of a man, a man like me? I am a man, a good, strong man, a man who simply wants to live in peace like other men, with his family, free.*

Now with his recall to Charlestown, and the sale of his son, Mark knew it was time to make his move. In the cramped garret where they slept, he began a hushed conversation with Phillis, "I think it's time for drastic measures. I can't be away from you any longer. It's hard labor that I'm at daily and it keeps getting worse, the hours on the docks get longer and longer. I never know who I'll be sent to work for and as cruel as the Cap'n is — those he loans me out to are worse. Cap'n gives no thought to you or me or our family, we may as well be the farm cattle. He gives more thought to his precious horse than to any of us. It wasn't so bad until Missus passed. Without her to settle him down and calm his moods, he's often in a dark place. I long to be free, Phillis, to live with you and the children, in peace, and in control of our lives." He paused, taking a deep breath and blinking back the tears, "I'm going to poison Cap'n Codman, Phillis."

Phillis, shaken by his words, stared intently into Mark's eyes, "What, Mark?"

"I'm going to poison the Cap'n, my love. Then we can be free."

"Mark…"

"I'll need your help, Phillis."

"What do you mean, Mark. I can't kill a man, even a man so mean as the Cap'n. And Mark…neither can you, can you?"

"I didn't think I could, honestly, Phillis, until he sold our boy…that was the last straw for me." Tears filled his eyes as he spoke, remembering the son they lost.

"But, Mark, are you sure?"

"There has to be a better way, Phillis…we need to escape this life and save what is left of our family and our life." He paused and added, "You know Phillis, you know it's been done before, we wouldn't be the first to succeed."

"I know we've all heard the stories, but Mark, if we get caught…" She couldn't bring herself to say the words. They both knew it meant death.

"I know, I know." Mark gently touched her hand, "but Phillis, if we do, we could be free. Why shouldn't we be able to accomplish what others have? Isn't it worth trying?"

"I don't know, Mark. I hate what you're going through…what we're going through…and I want to help you, truly I do, but Mark, to kill a man?"

"I'm worried, too. I'm afraid for your life," he stroked her cheek. "Look what happened to poor Tom, the Cap'n hit him so hard, he won't ever have the use of his eye again. You or I could be his next victim. I've already worked out a plan, Phillis. It's foolproof. We won't get caught, and then we'll be free or at the very worst, sold to a kinder master. Help me, please." He begged.

She looked at him, still shocked at his proposal. "We'll need Phoebe's help as well, or we'll surely be caught because most days she works the household with me."

"That's true. Do you think she'll join us?"

"I don't know, Mark, there could be a great gain, but, if we get caught, the cost will be even greater," her voice trembled as she spoke the words.

"It'll be okay, Phillis. We'll ask her tomorrow, when Quaco is here for his weekly visit. She'll have to tell her husband the plan anyway. He might as well hear it from us."

The next morning dawned and the slaves on the estate looked forward to their weekly visits with relatives and friends. Mark and Phillis approached their tasks with a mixture of anticipation and anxiety. Today they agreed they would enlist Phoebe's help with the plan.

Their duties done for the evening, Mark, Phillis, Phoebe, and Quaco gathered outside near the old oak tree. It was far enough from the main house and the other slave quarters they would not be heard.

After some casual conversation sharing news of the week, Mark began, "Phoebe, have you seen poor Tom? I talked to him today. He told me he still can't see out of the eye the Cap'n struck him in. It's hard for him, he's still having a lot of headaches and pain from the blow. He hasn't even been able to work much and is fearing the Cap'n might cast him out. Truth is I'm fear for all of us, one of us could be his next victim."

"I saw him early this morning. His face still bears the marks of the blow. It's sad for him. You think the Cap'n might cast him out with nothin'?"

"I wouldn't be surprised, you know he's done it in the past, when he feels slaves is past their usefulness." Mark paused, watching her reaction. "Phillis and I, we'd like to keep that from happenin' to you or to us, ya' know? Maybe it'll keep an injury like that at bay and a castin' out away. We'd like your help to carry it out, Phoebe, would ya' be willin'? Even knowin' it'd be dangerous, but it also might be the biggest opportunity of your life."

"What you planning now, Mark Codman?" Quaco interrupted. He had heard the story of Mark's earlier arson scheme and knew it too was a dismal failure.

"Shush…we planning to poison the Cap'n to gain our freedom, Quaco Dalton," came the fast, low reply.

"Poison the Cap'n? Are you out of your head? How you going to do that?" Phoebe joined in, surprised at Mark's revelation, but interested nonetheless.

"Yes, Phoebe, with the help of you and Phillis, I plan to poison the Cap'n and move on to a better place just like Salmon's slaves did."

"Phoebe, don't you listen to Mark Codman. He's gonna get you killed or worse!" Quaco touched her arm as he spoke, concerned for his wife and furious at Mark Codman for his blasted idea.

"Quaco Dalton, you hush, you ain't seen the dark moods of the Cap'n like we have. Tell me more, Mark. What exactly are you asking me to do?"

"Well, Phoebe, I need you to help Phillis administer the poison to the Cap'n's food and drink. He'll pass. The heirs will then either sell us or grant us our freedom."

"How's that gonna work? Where you gonna get poison anyhow?"

Well, you and Phillis, you know the Cap'n's eating schedule, the foods and drinks he likes, you can mix it in here and there without being seen. And as to the poison, I'll get it, you don't need to know where, and then we'll hide it well. The Cap'n will be gone before you know it and we'll be startin' a new life."

"How are you so sure this plan will work, Mark Codman? Last time I listened to one of your plans, you're the only one who got what he wanted!"

"The plan is foolproof this time, he'll take the poison, in his food, and he won't even know it. He'll be gone and his family will be none the wiser."

Quaco couldn't stand it any longer, "Mark Codman, you are going to get my wife killed! And on top of that, you know murdering is a sin. The Bible tells us so."

"I ain't planning to break any commandments, Quaco Dalton. If we don't lay hands on him or spill his blood, it ain't no sin."

"How do you figure?"

"It's all laid out in that book o' Numbers, in the chapter 35. As long as we don't hit him with an iron object, a stone, or a wooden post, in a vicious way, it ain't on the list of murders. That's what the Good Book says, I know 'cause I can read it. It's the one kind thing the Cap'n did for me – teaching me to read."

In Phoebe's mind that seemed to settle it, she wanted to help Mark, and she would love to be able to have more than a few hours with her husband, Quaco, every week. It also appeared to calm Phillis who hadn't even thought about breaking the commandments. But her Mark had, he had read it himself.

As Quaco and Phoebe walked away, Quaco wished he'd not been privy to the conversation. He knew of Mark's earlier attempt to acquire poison from the slave of a doctor and had warned the man against getting involved. Now his wife was to be a pawn in Mark's latest plot. Phoebe, unaware of his thoughts, walked alongside him dreaming of a better life.

Mark and Phillis headed for the garret to turn in for the night. As they walked, Mark whispered softly for Phillis' ears only, "I'll go to Robin on the morrow. He'll help me secure the poison and the plan will be underway. And a better life for us not far behind."

Phillis was still worried, though Mark seemed sure of his plan as well as Robin's complicity, he had talked to Robin on occasion about his ever evolving hopelessness and misery.

They had discussed the Salmon's slaves successful plan as well as the Barron poisoning that only a handful knew of.

As the slave of Dr. Clark, Robin had access to all the medicine in the Doc's apothecary. On top of that, Robin was legendary for his stand for freedom. Robin knew full well the devastation caused by the separation from loved ones that slaves experienced almost on a daily basis. His own family had been ripped apart when his Master Royall had passed and the family divvied up the property. His father had gone to the son, his mother along with he and his siblings had gone to the daughter. When she wed, they became the property of one Henry Vassall, her husband.

All went well for a while until Vassall ran into financial difficulties as a result of overindulging his only child, Margaret. He relieved the situation by selling Robin's sister and her children. Her husband was to remain with Vassall. She was pregnant at the time. When the child was born, her new master gave the baby away. Robin's sister was doubly devastated and her spirit completely broken. Worst of all, there was nothing he could do to help her.

Robin was later implicated in a robbery of a Vassall neighbor, Colonel William Brattle. Robin and the Colonel's slave stole a chest filled with wedding gifts including money and silver. They planned to take the chest, using the bounty within to escape to Nova Scotia and then to France. Their plan failed. They were caught and imprisoned. Robin's sentence was 20 lashes. The Colonel was given permission to dispose of Vassall's slave, Robin.

Today, Robin found himself enslaved by Dr. Clark. Still, in his heart was his belief he would one day escape the tyranny that was slavery and be free. His dream was the same as Mark's, to be his own man, to live his own life, beholden to no master. Mark had no doubt Robin would understand his plight and aid his cause. He would soon discover he was right and Robin was a willing accomplice to the goal of freedom.

Mark's state of desperation was evident when he visited Robin the following day. Mark knew that arsenic was toxic and would probably be the best choice to poison Captain Codman. He would only need a little to cause the Cap'n's death and it could easily be mixed into food or drinks without detection.

Foreseeing Mark's state, Robin had already stolen an ounce of arsenic from Dr. Clark. He'd carefully wrapped it in the white paper used in the apothecary and tied it with twine, just like Doc did.

The two conspirators met in the barn, out of sight, Robin handing off the tiny parcel to Mark with care. He had also brought along a measuring device fashioned from iron. Robin explained the process, "Use this measurer to put a tiny amount into an empty glass medicine vial, then add water. Stir it well, then mix it carefully with the Cap'n's food or drink. Mixed in just right, no one will be able to detect it, especially not the 'good ole Cap'n'."

"Are you sure this will work?" Mark replied, succumbing to the full measure of his plan.

"Yes, two doses should kill him even if he is strong."

"And you're sure his food won't taste any different?"

"No, it shouldn't 'cause arsenic doesn't taste peculiar, but just like cold water," Robin reassured him. "Remember the Salmon slaves succeeded last year with a similar plan, and so did the Barron slaves earlier this year." Robin didn't confess his role in either incident to Mark, but Mark now wondered if he had played a role in one or both of them.

Mark, calm and confident in his plan once more, slipped out of the barn unnoticed and headed back to the Codman mansion. When he arrived, he panicked when he realized he had lost the measuring device Robin had provided. He reassured himself when he realized he could fabricate a new one in the Blacksmith shop. He checked in with the Cap'n, making an excuse about needing to repair some hinges in the shop, and hastily hurried off to re-create the measurer. His task complete, he headed to the kitchen to find his accomplices.

Phillis and Phoebe were alone in the kitchen. The mistresses of the house, the Captain's eldest daughters, Elizabeth and Mary, had just departed, having given the orders for the day.

Mark showed them the measuring device and the arsenic, as he explained, "Measure a small amount and mix it in the glass vial with water. Then mix it with his drink or food when the opportunity arises. Use it every day 'til he's gone."

They measured the amount needed into the vial, mixed it with water and then carefully hid it in a corner of the kitchen closet where it would not be discovered. Phillis and Phoebe did all the cooking for the large household, so no one would inadvertently stumble upon the poison.

Mark departed to hide the remaining arsenic in the garret beneath the floorboards. Phoebe would hide the measuring device there later.

Their plan had begun.

Chapter 5

The Murder

Sunday, 22 June 1755

The slaves had no intention of harming anyone else in the household – only the Cap'n – for as they saw it, he alone was responsible for their dire circumstances.

Phillis and Phoebe planned to administer the first dose at tea time. The Cap'n himself did not drink tea, but an extravagant concoction of chocolate, herbs and spices, known simply as the "infusion." Like other men of his wealth and rank, his "infusion" featured imported cocoa beans revered for their stimulating properties.

The process to deliver it as he liked was long. Phoebe had begun the preparation the night before - grinding the cocoa beans on the grinding stone. Phillis prepared the boiling water over the fire. As usual, they added boiling water to the ground cocoa. Due to the heavy cocoa butter content, next she milled it and sweetened it with sugar, adding just the amount the Cap'n liked. Phoebe had then boiled the concoction once more, and taken it off the heat before heading to bed for the night.

It was to this concoction, that the poison would be introduced this morning. Phillis and Phoebe were up early, getting the kitchen fire started, listening to the orders of Mistresses Elizabeth and Mary. Once the ladies had departed, the poisoning began.

Phoebe milled the chocolate concoction once more, and set it on to boil, adding the arsenic as she stirred. She, then added the Cap'n's favorite spices – chili, cinnamon, and ginger - and left it to boil. She went about her tasks quietly, joining Phillis in preparing the family's breakfast. They baked bread, made fresh this morning, while heating the meat from last night's dinner. Amid the silence, Phoebe prepared berry pasties from the newly ripe blueberries picked yesterday. A hot porridge simmers on the fire.

As the breakfast comes together, Phillis mills the Cap'n's chocolate once more and pours it into his special silver pot as Phoebe pours the tea into the opulent tea pot for the rest of the family. Not a word is spoken between them from fear of giving away their secret.

They entered the dining area to see the Captain seated at his mahogany table awaiting his breakfast. The table was set earlier by Phillis and now it is she who begins to serve the meal to the Cap'n first, followed by the rest of the family who have not yet taken to their daily schedule. Mistresses Elizabeth and Mary stand behind their father, ready to give direction as needed to their slaves, who serve the breakfast with eyes downcast.

The Cap'n speaks to his sons regarding Tom, "What do you gentlemen feel should be done with Tom? He is not able to carry out his duties as he once was in the fields. Shall we set him out or shall we give him new duties with a different role?

John II, looked at his father, a bit bemused, yet not daring to mention the fact, that his father had been the one who had caused the damage to Tom, one of their most valuable slaves, "Well, we could take him off the fields and let him oversee the stores, Father. It would be less physically taxing, but one he should be able to do."

"Will his vision allow it, I wonder?" The Cap'n asked himself.

"I believe so, sir. He can still see with the one eye," The conversation is interrupted as Phillis fumbles the biscuits and Phoebe enters with the Cap'n's beverage.

Phoebe pours the Cap'n his chocolate. He sips it and gives a nod of approval. It is just as he likes it, otherwise he would have bellowed his disapproval. Mistress Elizabeth dismisses the slaves.

Phillis and Phoebe return with a sigh of relief. The first step is complete. They begin the process of cleaning, when Mark sticks his head in the door. They nod in unison. He nods back his praise and quickly slips back to his duties.

Later that evening, in the garret, Mark compliments his co-conspirators, "You all did a great thing today. The Cap'n, nor anybody else, has any idea. Soon, we'll all have a better life."

They both looked at him with no small amount of skepticism, "I hope you're right, Mark Codman," Phoebe offered, "I hope you're right."

Phillis merely smiled in support of her husband and prayed that he was indeed right.

Tuesday, 24 June 1755

Mark wasn't sure how long it would take for the poison to take its course and destroy the Cap'n, so he had planned another meeting with Robin for the morning, after all he might need more poison. That morning, Mark's instructions were to pick up some stoneware pots for Codman house over at potter John Harris' place. While there, he decided to buy a mug so he could gift Robin with a drink as a way to thank him for his assistance in the acquisition of the poison. In addition to the purchase of the mug, Mark also availed himself of galena, the lead sulfide used by potters for glazing and, of course, lethal if ingested.

Robin, believing it appropriate, disguised himself in a gentleman's black wig, and an elaborate blue topcoat with a yellow lining and upturned cuffs to meet Mark at the potter's. He had taken an early ferry from Boston and arrived in Charlestown before Mark.

Robin greeted Mark, "So, how goes it my friend?"

"All goes as planned, thank you," came Mark's reply followed by in a whisper, "Do you really feel that peacock camouflage is necessary?"

"Why yes, I have no cause to be in Charlestown today, and prudence is required, at least for myself."

Mark nodded his agreement.

Knowing discretion was still in order, they left the potter's separately and reunited at the Charlestown slaughterhouse where they walked together along the back lanes.

Near the long wharf, where the ferry launched for Boston, Mark slipped into the Widow Sherman's shop, ordered a drink to fill his mug, paid with Boston earnings (secretly withheld from the Cap'n on a regular basis) and returned to Robin who opted to wait outside. They shared the beverage lingering outside the Widow Sherman's discussing the news of the day, being careful not to mention the poison.

Unbeknownst to Mark, Captain Codman was out and about on Tuesday, taking the ferry to Boston to attend the launch of one of the ships in his fleet. On the ferry, he was approached by a farmer friend, who recognizing Codman, began, "Good Morning, Captain. What brings you out today?"

"Good Morning. I'm heading into Boston for a launch." About to dismiss the man, who approached him improperly, he was quickly interrupted.

"I have some information which might be of interest to you, Sir."

"What might that be?"

"Well, sir, it's valuable, maybe there's somethin' in it for me by sharing with you?"

"Not likely, sir, but proceed," The words, coated with disdain for this crude request rolled off the Cap'n tongue.

"Well, sir, I thought you might like to know that I just saw one of your slaves, Mark, drinking with another fellow, over by the Widow Sherman's." The farmer grinned, hoping this information might still curry him some favor with the wealthy Captain.

The Captain grimaced, "Thank you and good day, Sir."

The farmer huffed, "Good day, Captain," accepting his dismissal with as much dignity as he could muster.

Robin, who spent the remainder of the day in Charlestown running errands for Dr. Clark, found himself back at the long wharf, as the Captain was returning from Boston. He scurried out of sight, but carefully watched Codman enter the Widow Sherman's establishment. He approached the window with care, as he heard the Captain say, "Mrs. Sherman, you would do me a great service if you would no longer serve my slaves alcohol."

Taken aback by the Captain's abrupt approach, though seemingly polite, she responded, "Yes, sir," as if obeying a direct order – which is exactly what it was.

Mark had already arrived home, deposited the pots he'd picked up at the potter's and hid the galena in Codman's blacksmith shop – just in case.

Wednesday, 25 June 1755

Phoebe and Phillis continued their poisoning using all the arsenic Mark had supplied. Much to their dismay, the Cap'n was still up and about, feeling fine, and barking orders.

That evening, Phoebe voiced her disapproval, "What do we do now, Mark Codman? You told us he'd be gone after two doses! Did you see him today, he's his usual self, maybe even healthier," she exaggerated.

"It's true, Mark. It's not affecting him at all," Phoebe agreed.

"Don't worry. I'll tell Robin we need more. I'm sure he will help." Mark reassured them, all the while wondering to himself why it was taking so long to work. He was afraid to use the galena because its grittiness would be detected in food or drink. He'd think of an excuse to go to Boston tomorrow and ask Robin's help once again.

Thursday, 26 June 1755

On rising, Mark tells the Cap'n he must go to Boston for supplies for a project he's completing. He takes the ferry to Boston and heads straight to Dr. Clark's to see Robin. On arriving, Mark quietly makes his request, "Robin, the poison is not working as quickly as you told me…"

"Well, how much are you givin' the man, maybe you added too much water to the mix."

"No, it was measured just like you told me, I sure of it."

"Well, maybe the Cap'n's got so much meanness in him, it'll take more…" Robin laughed at his own joke, but then became serious, "I can't get you any more tonight without arousing the Doc. I'll deliver you more on the morrow."

"Thank you, my friend. You are saving my life."

Friday, 27 June 1755

Robin, in disguise, arrives after dark at the Codman mansion to make his clandestine delivery. Phillis sees him coming up the walk toward the kitchen, "Robin Vassall?" she questions.

"No'm," he replies, changing his voice, "I'm just a country Negro bringing news for Mark Codman, It's 'bout his son."

"His son is my son, what news?" As she pressed him further, a voice from inside called her back to work as the Cap'n was finally experiencing stomach ailments.

Robin looked 'round the estate, but failed to find Mark anywhere.

Meanwhile, Mark could not be found, as he had gone to meet Robin. He realized, too late, that they must've gotten their signals crossed regarding the meeting place. It was only much later they would discover; they had missed each other twice on the ferry that night.

Saturday, 28 June, 1755

Mistresses Elizabeth and Mary entered the kitchen as Phillis prepared the breakfast and Phoebe was scraping the rust off a cast iron pot. She paused to wipe the sweat from her brow as Mistress Elizabeth spoke, "Phoebe, I dare say Father will be having porridge again for breakfast. I fear he is not quite himself again today."

Phillis answered, "Yes, miss, I'll prepare some for him, right away. I'm sure he'll be improving today and back to his old self shortly. You know how strong your father is, ma'am."

"Thank you, Phillis. You are very kind." Elizabeth smiled weakly and left the kitchen.

So, the Cap'n is getting worse, Phoebe grinned to herself and got back to her pot, saying nothing.

And Phillis finally relaxed, believing for the first time that the plan might just work.

Later that day, porringer was again requested for the Cap'n's dinner. Phillis took the opportunity to add the remaining arsenic to the porringer before serving him.

Meanwhile, Mark headed back into Boston to try and procure more arsenic from Robin. He found Robin sitting outside of Dr. Clark's in Boston's North End. Again, he requested additional arsenic.

"I can't get it for you now, Mark. You'll have to wait 'til the Sabbath."

Mark agreed and with permission remained in Boston that night.

Sunday, 29 June 1755

Mark attended the Sabbath services, as required. He spoke briefly with Robin and they agreed to meet later that evening for the exchange.

Under cover of darkness, on the Sabbath, the exchange was made. Mark spent another restless night in Boston, planning to return to the mansion early the next morning.

Mark's arrival at the Codman mansion was greeted with news of the master's condition – severe vomiting and diarrhea. Mark quickly rushed to the garret to hide the arsenic, to be mixed and used later that day.

Mark scurried back to the kitchen, arriving just in time to hear the Mistresses instructing Phoebe and Phillis to serve the Cap'n sago – an East Indian starchy gruel – for his breakfast. As they went about making the necessary preparation to serve the Cap'n in his bedchamber, Mark found himself alone in the kitchen. He quickly grabbed the galena from its hiding place and added some to the gruel boiling over the fire. It would have to do; he couldn't get the arsenic in that moment. He hoped it would speed the Cap'n's death and keep him from suffering more.

Moments later, Phillis and Phoebe were ready to serve him. They gathered the necessary accoutrements and headed upstairs where they found Mistresses Elizabeth and Mary at the Cap'n's side. They served the gruel and stepped outside the room, listening before returning to the kitchen.

Codman, even in his weakened state, complained, "This sago is gritty. Are those slaves falling down on their service because I am ill?"

Phillis and Phoebe quickly departed, afraid, before hearing anymore of the conversation. Mark had not told them he added the galena.

After all the arsenic and now the galena, much to Mark's surprise and dismay, the Captain did not die that night.

Tuesday, 1 July 1755

Phillis and Phoebe were met early in the kitchen by the mistresses, whose appearance indicated they'd had little sleep. Again they requested the sago for their father.

As the mistresses returned to their father, a knock at the door deferred them from their mission. It was Doctor Clark, coming to check on his friend.

"Oh, Doctor Clark, thank you for coming to check on Father, we've tried the usual remedies, but nothing is working, and he is getting weaker." Miss Elizabeth explained the situation and together they led Doctor Clark to their father's room.

On entering, the Cap'n rallied at the sight of his friend, "William, what the hell brings you here?"

"Why you, of course, Cap'n John, word reached me in Boston that you were a bit under the weather, what ails you, my friend."

"Just some stomach troubles, maybe a bit too much rich food or maybe overindulgence of the infusion…"

"But, Father…" Elizabeth tried to interrupt, but was cut off.

"Girls, why don't you leave your father with me for a few minutes while I examine him."

Meanwhile in the kitchen, Phillis and Phoebe prepared the sago, adding their special ingredient – arsenic. When it reached the desired consistency, they carried it upstairs to the Cap'n.

Knocking at the door, they were surprised to be greeted by Doc' Clark.

"'Scuse us, Doctor Clark, we were bringing the Cap'n his dinner."

"Why, I just finished my examination, please bring it in, he could use some sustenance."

Turning to John, William said, "Take care, my friend, I'll leave the elixir with the girls, it's up to you to take it though. I'll let myself out. Be well."

And with that he was gone, but not fast enough for Phoebe and Phillis.

Even with the Doc's elixir, Mark, Phillis, and Phoebe didn't have long to wait this time. Within hours, the Cap'n succumbed to convulsions and finally to death. The deed was done. They had succeeded. The Captain was dead. Would they now be free?

Chapter 6

The Law

Mark slept fitfully that night. He woke many times wondering why the peaceful sleep he imagined so many times would not come.

Phillis was no better, finally awakening with a muffled scream, which Mark suppressed further. It would do no good for the mourning family to hear unseemly screams from the garret where they slept. He tried to settle her, but it was no use.

Soon Phoebe started, wide awake and covered in a cold sweat. Their eyes gazed at one another, trying to show courage and relief but instead mirroring only worry and trepidation. What if they were caught? They knew the punishment and it overcame them as they each fell back into their own thoughts, back into the erratic, restless sleep of guilt and fear.

Precedents had been set and the powers that be in Boston would see that they were punished to the fullest extent of the law if they were caught. They all knew it well and the rest of the night was filled with horrifying dreams of the slaves who affected rebellion and the punishment heaped upon them when they were convicted.

Try as he might, Mark tried to think of the Salmon slaves and how they got away with murder and moved on to a better life. Instead, he dreamed of the slave insurrection on the Danish Island of St. John. The slaves on St. John, the

Akan people who had been stolen from their homeland, suffered innumerable illnesses, severe slave codes, and countless droughts. Their dreadful suffering forced the Akan leadership to plot rebellion against their masters. A small number of the conspirators smuggled in weapons and killed Danish soldiers at the fort on Coral Bay plantation. Soon after, they were joined by 150 more collaborators, who attacked on the other island plantations, killing white colonists. Their attack surprised the colonists and allowed the slaves to take command of a large portion of the island claiming it as their own for six short months. The following spring, hundreds of French troops landed on St. John and put down the rebellion in violent fashion with extreme prejudice. Mark's dreams put him in the midst of the conspirators – a dead man. It was the last thing he expected after the success of his plot.

Phillis suffered through her own night of dread. Her nightmare took her to Jemmy's rebellion at the Stono River in South Carolina, where Jemmy and a band of slaves seeking freedom from their captors. She could almost smell the burning buildings as the insurgents broke into the Hutchenson store, killing the store's white owners, cutting off their heads and showcasing them on the stores steps. Their rampage moved on killing colonists, burning houses and businesses intent on reaching Spanish Florida where they would achieve the liberty they longed for so desperately. What had begun as a small rebellion of near 20 soon reached numbers of 100 or more. For almost a week they marched, crying out for liberty, fighting off the colonists and supporting English troops when suddenly the rebellion was crushed with the death of nearly every one of the conspirators. Phillis tossed and turned as the nightmare played out in her head – she could not shake the feeling that her own path to liberty would soon end in her death.

Phoebe was not immune to the fear that had also overcome her co-conspirators. They had murdered their master with high hopes of freedom and now as night had fallen she seemed to feel the fires burning slowly creeping up her body – if caught she could be truly burning or suffer a fate worse than death – hard labor at one of the horrid Indies plantations torn from her husband forever. Her terrifying dreams carried her to New York City where slaves purportedly burned Fort George in its entirety. Fires, then, sprung up all over the city in rebellion against the whites who continually tormented and tortured every soul of African descent. She could hear the whites screaming that slaves had set the fires spurred to revolt by priests and their Catholic followers. The authorities quickly concluded a resistance was afoot and likely included the Papa peoples, the Igbo tribes, the Malagasy, and the "Cuba Peoples" – all enslaved people who groaned for the freedoms they had lost when torn from their homes. She could see the boy, about 16, an indentured servant, Joe he was called, claiming knowledge of the incredible plot to help himself out of a tight spot in the New York gaol. He told the magistrate the slaves were in cahoots with several white insurgents and the plan to was kill white males, capture white women and children, and burn the city to the ground. To protect the whites, numbering 7,000, from the blacks numbering 1,700 plus, the city's officials descended on the city arresting those believed to be involved in the plot. At the end of the manhunt, 30 black male slaves along with four whites (two men and two women) were executed after a speedy trial. In addition, 70 slaves were forced into further exile, still enslaved around the globe. Later 17 more slaves were hanged while 13 were burned at the stake. Phoebe was terrified of her fate should she be caught and wondered "why on earth did I listen to Mark Codman?" And she even allowed her mind to wander, "if the authorities come for me, is there any way out?"

Even she knew the law, as property she had no rights. If caught, there would be a trial, but a trial with no defense. If found guilty, the end was near, there was no hope.

Meanwhile, below them, in the main portion of the house, the surviving Codman family could not find rest either. Though they had all resigned to their quarters in the mansion, sleep would not come, as questions filled their mind and echoed through the halls, "How could this happen?" Shock and sadness was the order of the night.

Mary and Elizabeth, though retired, could not stop the tears, they had been the apple of their father's eye, taking charge of the house when their mother had passed. They were truly heartbroken at his loss.

The word had gone out following their father's death that morning. Mistresses Elizabeth and Mary had seen to it that the news of his passing was shared throughout Charlestown and Boston. As their doors were knocked on and the news shared, extended family, friends, and neighbors were shocked by the news that Captain John Codman was dead.

John, II, with the assistance of his brothers, had respectfully prepared their father's body in the early afternoon. Breaking with the tradition of the shroud, they had made the unanimous decision to bury the Captain in his full military regalia. Mark had been sent to the goldsmith with a written order for the mourning rings to be given to family and close friends following the funeral. They would be gold with an inscription that included the Captain's name and the dates of his birth and death. The rings served as a reminder of human mortality and eternity to come.

Mark had also been tasked by the heirs with a stop at the cabinet maker, to provide the dimensions required for the Captain's coffin. The goldsmith and the cabinet maker, knowing the Captain's rank and anticipating a bonus for expedient, quality work, set aside other projects and promised to deliver their wares by sundown the following day. It was a tall order, but it could be done.

As the body was prepared, Mistresses Elizabeth and Mary directed Phillis and Phoebe in the preparation of the front parlor where the Captain's body would be placed once the coffin arrived. Mourners would pay their last respects to the Captain there. The mirrors and paintings in the home were shrouded in white fabric as was the custom to show respect to their father.

****

In addition to the preparation, a coroner's inquest had been ordered and was to take place on the morrow. Each member of the family tried to gain rest, but shock soon gave way to questions regarding their father's death that simply had to be answered. Sleep finally came for each of the Codman heirs, but restful it was not.

John II and his siblings woke early, understanding the need for preparation and propriety that accompanied their rank in Boston society. Their servants, and unbeknownst to them, the murderers of their father, had risen even earlier, working to hide their fear and carry on their duties. The parlor preparation had to be completed, the family had to be fed, and food preparations for the mourners' visits had to be begun. Under the instruction of Elizabeth and Mary, Phillis and Phoebe went to work. Breakfast was prepared and served to the family with care.

Next, the black Wedgewood tea services were taken down, polished, and set out for service. Rosemary and tansy were placed in vases around the mourning parlor to counter the scent of death that had already begun to permeate the mansion. The coffin would set atop a table placed for that sole purpose. The body would lay in the parlor for two days, one day for viewing and a second day to determine that the 'deceased' would not recover. Ironically, embalming was not practiced in the colony, but rather arsenic was sprinkled both inside and outside of the body to kill bacteria and insects.

As breakfast was finished the coroner's jury members arrived and began their work. Mark, nervously watched as they arrived, trying to convince himself they were still in the clear. Phillis and Phoebe were alerted to their presence by the call for tea service for the gentlemen. Under the direction of John Remington, Coroner, the jury members went quickly about their work, presented with the task of discovering when, by what means, and how Captain John Codman died.

They spent most of the day wrapped up in their investigation. The longer they lingered, the more nervous Mark, Phillis, and Phoebe became, but they had to go about their work as normally as they could.

Among the other Codman slaves, along with slaves from the neighboring manors, rumors ran rampant. Many had heard Mark's complaining about the Cap'n's treatment, and his constant cries for freedom, but only a few knew of his plot to murder the Cap'n.

Now those who had heard the rumors, wondered had he really gone through with it? They had heard the same stories as Mark, the stories of the freed Salmon slaves and the murder that had set them free.

The slaves watched and listened with bated breath to hear the next tidbit of news and more importantly to see if indeed there had been a murder and if so who was the perpetrator.

In the meantime, the coffin arrived, embellished with hinges, handles, and a decorative silver plate from the Revere Silver Shop. It was set up in the front parlor. The Captain's body was gently placed by his sons with his right hand upon his left and situated just beneath his ribcage in the posture of prayer. His daughters quickly hung the silk festoons around the coffin and place the diamond shaped decorative hatchment above the body for adornment.

The mourning jewelry was delivered and the pastor arrived to comfort the family and offer prayers on their behalf. The funeral itself would follow tomorrow morning. Mourners began arriving and the servants placed the food prepared for them, serving as each wave arrived and preparing more food as the day went forward.

The coroner's jury completed their work and returned to Charlestown to prepare their report. Under oath, each of the 16 men signed sworn statements which declared that Captain John Codman had died by poison.

The official report was kept quiet out of respect for the family until the following afternoon after the funeral and burial had taken place. They hoped to lull the murderer or murderers into a sense of security and prevent any attempt of escaping justice.

*****

The morning of the funeral dawned bright and clear. The family donned mourning clothes, in the form of black capes and hats adorned with black ribbon for ladies and black armbands for the gentlemen. Guests would be attired in like fashion.

A feast was prepared for the friends and family who would come to pay their respects. The minister arrived, the mourners gathered and the service began on the grounds of the mansion. Prayers offered, the coffin was closed and nailed closed. The coffin was lovingly covered with the traditional black cloth pall and the pallbearers lifted it and carried it with care to the family burial grounds where the Captain would join his beloved wife.

Ahead of the coffin, mourning banners were carried and also followed behind and just before the Codman family. The family followed the coffin, each bearing their grief in their own way. Behind the family, the mourners, family, friends, and neighbors walked in pairs toward the newly dug grave.

The Codman slaves followed, permitted to attend in the background of the internment. Mark, Phillis, and Phoebe stood among them. Each had tears in their eyes, certainly not for the loss of the Cap'n, but rather for the family and the loss they were suffering at the hands of those they had trusted. It lent both an air of gullibility, coupled with culpability, to the murderers, though the family was as yet unaware of the betrayal.

The minister offered a final prayer for the captain as the coffin was eased into the earth as the family cast sprigs of rosemary into the grave. It was then covered – laying the 'ceased in his final resting place.

The tombstone would soon follow, being placed at the tain's head to mark his final resting place. It would be a moc ombstone, one adorned with a winged cherub in the Biblic adition, intended to ward off demons and plead for the merc God in the afterlife. Death, as it was, was a common occurrence in the colony, where the average life span was only 46. The Captain had beaten the odds, only to have his life stolen from him.

The family, followed by those who had come to pay their respects, returned to the mansion for the feast prepared by Phillis and Phoebe, as well as other slaves loaned to the Codman's for the day to serve the large number in attendance at the funeral. The feasting continued into the evening, as those in attendance offered their condolences and shared fond memories of the Captain with his surviving family.

In attendance that day, were a number of the Boston elite including Stephen Sewell, Chief Justice, as well as Chambers Russell, Benjamin Lynde, and John Cushing, all Associate Justices. Also paying their respects to the Codman clan that day were Dr. William Clark (as well as his many of his dock tenants), Thaddeus Mason, the Attorney Genera' William Stoddard, the Justice of the Peace, Samuel Ad rising politician and neighbor, and Paul Revere. Phi' Phoebe noted that day a number of the highest-officials of the colony. As guests began to depart, John Codman, II, along with his wife and his eldest sisters, thanked them for their attendance and offered each a token of the golden mourners' rings they had prepared for this day.

As the day wore on, the Codman family connections caused the fear Mark, Phillis, and Phoebe felt rise to a crescendo. Nearly every connection to the family owned slaves just as the Codman's did, and that in itself meant if they were caught in their little conspiracy – there would be no mercy.

Chapter 7

The Confession

The next days passed quietly as John Codman II slowly began to take over the affairs of his deceased father. The court appointed viewers had come following the funeral to take inventory of the estate for probating and valuing. The will was read shortly after and John Codman II took his rightful place as the heir and now family head.

Though still in mourning, business had to be attended to for the good of the entire family. Of particular concern was the tea trade as a large portion of the family's business was tied up there. The colonies consumed more than 2,000,000 pounds of tea per year and though the British monopolized the trade and made the East India Company leaders very rich, some colonists in Boston had begun to voice their displeasure and rebel discretely against the Crown and its control.

The good Captain was among those who joined in the rebellion by purchasing tea from the Dutch, who offered tea to the colonials at considerably lower prices than their British competition. The Crown was furious, allowing prices to continue to rise and now there was even talk of a tax reaching the ears of the colonists. In addition, the British Navy intensified its efforts to stop the colonial smugglers who were purchasing tea from the Dutch.

John II knew he would have to quickly apprise himself of his father's affairs to keep the estate solvent and continue to grow the family's wealth. He soon found himself amid discussions with Dr. Clark, Chambers Russel, Paul Revere, Samuel Adams, John Hancock, and other members of Boston society who met secretly to discuss, not only tea and the impending tax, but the growing infringements on their freedoms.

Seeing his new master, John Codman II so busy at work, lulled Mark into a sense of security which overflowed to Phillis and Phoebe. There had been little talk in the house of the cause of the Captain's death, the family continued in mourning, but went about their daily duties as expected.

Occasionally Mark found himself in somewhat of a panic. There were slaves who knew of the plot: Robin, of course, who had helped him, as well as Essex, the supplier of potter's galena. Phoebe's husband, Quaco, also knew. Mark knew him to have a flapping tongue, but felt secure that he would keep quiet if only for the sake of his Phoebe. In that knowledge Mark lulled himself back to a sense of calm.

The fears would again rise as Phillis and Phoebe heard gossip from the other Codman slaves. Lots of questions were being asked, and many theories as to what happened to the Cap'n, but for the most part, life had been easier the last few days with new master Codman in charge, and they were content in knowing the Cap'n was gone.

The morning of 6 July, 1755, dawned bright, with high humidity. In front of the magistrates in Boston stood young David Park, trembling with fear, tears streaming down his face. David, 18, reluctantly placed his left hand on the Bible, slowly raising his right as instructed. A long silence engulfed the court room as the magistrates took a solemn glance at his right hand. Ordered to "swear to tell the truth, so help me God," David complied, knowing he would need all the help God would give him that day.

The words he spoke seemed to fall on deaf ears, as his right hand told a story the judges heard loud and clear. Burned into David's right thumb was the capitol letter "T" calling him out as a thief for all to see. It was the evidence they needed, evidence of his previous conviction in a court case many miles and years away in London.

In this courtroom of Oyer and Terminer, past convictions were held in great esteem, an indicator of the accused as a confirmed malefactor. Implanted directly from London, this was the standard the court used for the now infamous witch trials years ago. Today, in 1755, the court enforced criminal, religious, and political laws, empowered to "hear and determine" as it were all cases – from treason to felony to misdemeanor – punishing as it deemed appropriate.

As the court saw it, David had been given leniency back in London, during the trial of his first offense. A local pastor offered David his support and pleaded for leniency when the then 14-year-old was accused of stealing from a London shopkeeper. In spite of the pastor's efforts, David was convicted of the theft.

In light of his crime, with a painful brand on his right hand, David was offered two unimaginable choices – seven years in prison or seven years of indentured servitude in America. The courts in London often offered this choice in order to reduce the population of poor and undesirables in London. It also provided laborers needed in the Americas. In many cases, a choice was not given, convicts were simply sent into a lifetime of indentured servitude with no hope of freedom.

There were even those in London and the surrounding area who sold themselves into servitude in hopes of a better life in the New World. Their contracts were for a time period of four to seven years in which time the servant would receive room, board, and training in a colonial trade as their payment.

David knew full well the conditions in the London prisons. He chose the latter, seven years of servitude in America had to be a better choice than seven years in prison where he would likely die of disease or starvation. At least in America, he might learn a trade and at the end of his sentence make a life for himself.

David remembered his choice well, but now, here in this Boston Court, he knew there would be no leniency. He had no family, not here, not in London. No one would presume him innocent, as the branded "T" silently testified against him. There were no supporting witnesses to come forward on his behalf. There would be no council for David, for none dared tarnish their reputations by pleading leniency on this, his second offense.

The Boston court, presided over by William Stoddard, understood its responsibility – to eliminate ideological and criminal elements from the Massachusetts Colony and maintain order. The court wielded all the power – even execution – and would not hesitate to use that unlimited power as it saw fit.

Would they in his case, David wondered? He had lived here for four years and knew that each and every sentence handed down was a public spectacle, encouraged by the political and religious leaders in an effort to control the public and deter criminal behavior.

David felt his best, really his only option, was to confess his crime and beg for the court's mercy. Confess he did. His tears flowed as he told of his visit to the Revere family shop, the pocketing of a small silver spoon and cup, when he was momentarily left alone there the temptation overwhelmed him. He blamed it on the beauty of the items, as well as the knowledge they could be sold or traded easily for food and provisions. He apologized for his lack of judgement and even asked the magistrates to please consider the fact that for four years he had been on the straight and narrow, learning the leather trade successfully. Would they offer him any mercy?

He waited nervously, as the judges deliberated. David knew the possible penalties – execution, banishment, whipping, time in the stocks, or pillaring. The court was well aware that labor in the colonies was in short supply and this, in itself, swayed them from execution and banishment.

The sentence came quickly. First would come the whipping post, then the stocks and pillory. All were located in the city center, the perfect stage for the entire community to observe and be involved in his punishment.

Suddenly, like lightning, a thought came flashing into his head. He quickly spoke, "Honored sirs, can I speak, just one more time?"

Judge Stoddard answered, "What else could you possibly have to say?"

"Sir, I have some news of a slave uprising…I don't know…but would it be of any use to you?"

Stoddard looked severely at young David Park. Was this a ruse, he wondered? An opportunity to delay his punishment? Stoddard offered an inquiring look to his fellow magistrates. They quickly nodded their agreement, though Stoddard had asked no question aloud.

Motioning to the bailiff, Stoddard ordered the removal of David Park from the courtroom to Stoddard's chambers. The bailiff quickly acted, depositing David in the judge's office and remaining at his side. The magistrates followed as hastily as possible.

Within the secure walls of the chamber, Stoddard began, "Mr. Park, what information do you possess that might be useful to us?"

David, hesitated momentarily, but then spoke promptly, after all he had nothing to lose and potentially much to gain. "I know I am facing the whipping post, plus probably the stockade and pillory, and then continued time as an indentured servant with time added for this incident. I ask that you sirs have mercy on me, if'n what I tell you be helpful in solving a crime committed lately by some slaves. If after you hear it, it is o' no value, let me accept my punishment without no further questions.

Stoddard admittedly was skeptical as David spoke, but something within told him to hear the young servant's story. He glanced again for the other's consent which they gave in silent nods.

"We agree. Tell your tale."

"You know, sirs, that my trade as a tanner takes me all 'round the area, working to supply leather for boots, shoes, doublets, jerkins, and also saddles and bridles for the gentry as well as the farmers. Many of you have seen me on your property and know I do good work in my trade."

"We do. But let's get along to the evidence you have, if there is any." Sarcasm dripped from Judge Stoddard's words.

"Yes, your honor, several months back I was at the home of Mr. Dalton, where I delivered leather to his man, Quaco, to be made into a new saddle for his Master. Quaco was upset some' terrible the morning of my arrival. It was strange as he'd just come from visiting his wife, Phoebe. I greeted him and queried to his health. He simply said he was fine, but confessed he was worried for his wife. When I asked why, he quieted for a short time, but then it was as if something burst from within and he started a yammering things I wished I hadn't heard.

He told me his wife belonged to Cap'n Codman, who like everyone, I knew was a man with a sore temper."

Seeing the magistrates' faces, David paused, and then apologized, "No offenses meant, sirs."

"Go on, David," Stoddard remarked intrigued and still mourning the loss of his friend, the John Codman. What

David did not know, though the magistrates did, was the coroner's jury had found the Captain was dead of poison, though no one – yet – knew how or by whom the deed was done. Rumors had flown, the children did it to gain their inheritance, or the slaves reacted violently as a result of the purported maltreatment of one of their own at the hands of the Captain.

As Stoddard pondered, David continued, "Quaco kept on talking, telling me the tale of Tom, one of the Cap'n's men who had been struck so hard on the face, he had lost his sight. I don't know the details, but Quaco seemed to fear the same fate might come to his Phoebe. When I asked him if that was it, he said no, and boy, was I wrong in what I thought." David stopped to take a breath, and because he could see the justices were fully enthralled in his tale.

"Well, what was it?" Stoddard snapped.

"Sir, he then tells me the Cap'n's man, Mark, was planning to poison him, so's he could get a new master.

Worse than that, sirs, Mark had the help of the house slaves, Phillis and Quaco's own wife, Phoebe.

"How did this Quaco know all this, Park?"

"He heard it straight from the horse's mouth, sir, Mark himself. Two nights prior, Mark had laid out his plan to Phillis, Phoebe, and Quaco, who was there for his weekly married visit, sir."

"How did this Mark plan to undertake this poisoning? Where would he get poison from? Are you sure you have this right, Park? I know personally Mark was the Captain's most trusted servant."

"Sirs, Quaco told me Mark laid out the plan likewise – to get the poison from Doc Clark's man, Robin, who he'd already spoke to, and then have the women give the poison to the Captain in his food and kill him. Quaco said Mark didn't see no fault in it – 'cause the Bible says it ain't no murder as long as no blood is shed."

"So, let me get this straight, David, Mark masterminded this plan, and Phillis, Phoebe, and Quaco agreed to it?"

"Oh no sir, Quaco told Mark to stop his foolishness, cause if he were caught, they'd all be dead. Quaco told his Phoebe straight out, not to go along with the plan, that Mark was going to get her killed if she did. He was rightly scared though, 'cause Phillis was going to do it for Mark's sake and he thought Phoebe might too, the way Mark was promising them how they'd be free or sold to a kinder master if they helped him to do the deed."

"You do know that Captain Codman is dead, don't you?

"Yes, sir, I heard it was so. Does this help, sirs?"

The magistrates sat in silence, evaluating what David Park had divulged. Stoddard ordered him removed from the room. The bailiff complied leading David out. David was again fearful; would they believe his story? Was what Quaco told him even true? He knew the Captain was dead and had even heard some of the rumors, but rumors always circulated in the city and that didn't always make them true.

In moments, the magistrates called the bailiff and David back into the office. Stoddard spoke for the court, "David Park, mercy is temporarily granted you by this court, you will remain imprisoned until we can verify your story. If it proves to be true, restitution will be made by you to the Reveres for the stolen goods, and you will return to your master with only the remaining three years of your original agreement in place. If your story is shown to be false, your original sentence will be doubled. Do you understand?"

"Yes, sir. Sir, thank you, sirs." The bailiff followed the instruction to the letter, David Park was placed in a cell alone, David was thankful, at least he had saved his own skin if only temporarily.

*****

The magistrates acted quickly, knowing the information they now had in their possession, complements of indentured servant David Park, could solve the murder of their friend and colleague, Captain John Codman.

Chapter 8
The Inquiry

Justice Stoddard took the lead, calling the members of the Coroner's Jury together to further question their findings in light of this new testimony - compliments of indentured servant, David Park. Each man – Josiah Whitmore, Richard Deavens, Samuel Larkin, William Thompson, Samuel Kettle, Nathanial Brown, Thomas Larkin, John Larkin, Barnabas Davis, David Cheever, Benjamin Brazier, Edward Goodwin, Richard Phillips, Samuel Sprague, Michael Brigden, and Samuel Hendley – appeared before the court as requested by Justice Stoddard. In addition, Stoddard requested a consultation of both Doctor Clark and Doctor Gibbons.

After questioning the Coroner's Jury members regarding the oath they had sworn to regarding Codman's poisoning, the doctors were tasked with explaining the potential use of arsenic as a murder weapon.

Dr. Clark begins, "Honorable Magistrates, as you know arsenic is a heavy black metal mined from the earth, a substance you all know as highly toxic. It is distilled into a white powder for multiple uses. Arsenic's most common uses are as an additive in glass making, pottery making, paints, dyes, and even as an ingredient in rat poison. Medicinally it has shown some promise in the smallest of doses in the treatment of syphilis."

Dr. Gibbons, interrupts Dr. Clark, adding, "It is difficult to detect as a poison, mainly because arsenic poisoning and small pox have such similar symptoms – convulsions, difficulty breathing, diarrhea, vomiting, severe stomach pain, pale skin with evident lesions, seizures, followed by a coma state prior to death."

Dr. Clark offers, "That is true, Gibbons, and on top of all that arsenic looks like sugar or flour and is completely undetectable if given in small doses especially in hot foods and drinks. The only sign it gives at all is a garlic odor on the victim's breath and skin, and since it is used following death in preparation for burial to destroy bacteria, it is more difficult to discern arsenic poisoning, thus making it an ideal choice as a murder weapon."

As the justices and jury members listen intently, Dr. Gibbons continues, "As many of you know, arsenic is nicknamed the widow's poison and the inheritor's powder, and for good reason – given sparingly over weeks and months at a time it would likely never be detected. Of course, too much, too fast would cast suspicion on those closest to the victim or those with access to the victim's food and beverages – as is the case here."

Stoddard interrupts the doctors' discourses, "Doctor Clark, Doctor Gibbons, is there any way, in your opinion, to prove the slaves named by David Park are the perpetrators of the crime against Captain Codman?"

"Not by arsenic, sir, not without a confession," Clark interjects.

"But what about the potter's lead, the galena, we discovered at the testament of the Captain's daughters? They both gave testimony of the gritty substance remaining in the bowl after the Captain had finished his last meal, and so it was found.

"And what about the garlic scent pervading the Captain's body, though he had eaten nothing but sago for days, there's no garlic in that dish, your honors?" questioned Josiah Whitmore, a member of the Coroner's Jury and a friend of the late Captain.

The magistrates looked at one another, the same questions in their own minds. After a few moments, Justice Stoddard is the first to speak, "It appears, gentlemen, we will just need to coax a confession and then let justice take its course. We will begin with this Quaco, the property of James Dalton, who seems to be in the know and we will proceed from there."

*****

12 July 1755

Early on the morning of the 12th, the day dawned clear, as Mr. Dalton sat eating his breakfast. A knock at the door brought an officer of the court with a summons. On opening it, Dalton sees it is a call for his slave Quaco to appear before the court immediately for questioning.

Dalton is surprised at the summons, Quaco has caused him no problems thus far, even with his so-called wife living on the Codman estate. A thought dawns on Dalton, could this have something to do with Captain Codman's death? The rumors have been flying that slaves poisoned the Captain, but surely not, why would his Quaco want to murder the Captain?

Dalton quickly summons Quaco and decides it is best if he escort him to the court. He wants no trouble with the authorities.

Dalton arrives with Quaco at the Court and his presence is made known to the magistrates. Justice Stoddard once again takes lead, and has the slave, known as Quaco, brought in for examination.

"Quaco, please identify yourself," Stoddard begins.

"I am Quaco, my master is Mr. Dalton, there, sir," Quaco responds respectfully.

"Quaco, a witness has come forward stating that you may have knowledge of the death by poison of Captain John Codman, is this true?"

Quaco hesitates, thinking, contemplating his answer, considering how to tell the truth and still save his wife, Phoebe from death.

"Quaco, you will answer the question," Stoddard demands.

Quaco, fearful, begins slowly, carefully measuring his words, "Yes, sir…this winter past, Kerr, a Negro belonging to Doc Gibbons told me that Mark, a Negro belonging to Cap'n Codman, had come to him and asked for poison. Sir, I asked Kerr if Phoebe had been with Mark. Phoebe, that's my

wife, sir. Kerr Gibbons said no, only Mark had come and

asked him for the poison."

"Did this Kerr give Mark the poison he requested,

Quaco?"

"No, sir. I don't believe he did. But sir, I asked

Phoebe, Cap'n Codman's house Negro, my wife, when I saw

her on the next Saturday if she had been with Mark to get

some poison. She told me no. And then I warned her to be

wary of Mark Codman, that he could get her into big trouble.

I told her not have anything to do with that Mark Codman,

his poison, or his schemes."

"Good Quaco, do you know if Mark Codman ever

got his poison or what he wanted it for?"

"No sir, not really, sir, though I did hear Mark say he

would try to get poison somewhere else, maybe from Dr.

Clark's Negro, Robin."

*****

News traveled fast. No sooner had Quaco's Master Dalton taken him to the court than the news spread through the slaves' network to Phoebe that he had been taken in by the authorities. Panic overcame her. She sought out Phillis, who had already heard the news. Phillis tried in vain to calm Phoebe and herself. Who would be next? Where was Mark? They needed his guidance and protection now as surely as ever, after all this had all been his idea. Later in the day, they heard rumors that Kerr had been taken in by the authorities for questioning, and Robin Clark had been arrested in conjunction with the poisoning of the Cap'n.

Their fear continued to rise exponentially, especially since it seemed Mark was nowhere to be found. Had he been taken to?

Little did they know that Mark was working down at the docks today, sent there by their new master John Codman II. Mark, down on the docks, heard the rumors flying, but at this point was not concerned for there was no way the poison could be traced back to him because Phoebe and Phillis had been the ones to give it directly to the Cap'n – or so he thought.

*****

Meanwhile, the magistrates were moving quickly forward with their inquiries. First, they summoned Dr. Gibbons regarding his man Kerr. Kerr was promptly dispatched to meet with Justice Stoddard. After questioning, Kerr Gibbons was released back to his master with no evidence to incriminate him in providing any poison to Mark Codman.

Simultaneously, Robin, the Negro belonging to Dr. Clark, was arrested and charged as an accessory in the poisoning of Captain John Codman and subsequently delivered to the Boston Gaol. His examination would come later.

*****

Quaco had no idea, though he had tried to spare her, that his testimony had incriminated his wife, Phoebe. Quietly, the magistrates put a plan in motion to bring her in for questioning while not arousing the suspicions of Mark Codman, who they now believed to be the mastermind behind the plan to poison and kill his master, Captain John Codman.

A message was sent to John Codman II, explaining that Phoebe was needed for questioning in the matter of his father's death. He was told she could possibly have information regarding who obtained and administered the poison causing his father's death. Codman was to deliver her to the court on 19 July 1755 for questioning.

He had heard the rumors, just like everyone else, but could not believe his father had been poisoned by his trusted slaves.

19 July 1755

Phoebe had lived in terror for the last week, even though Quaco had tried his best to reassure her at their sole Saturday night visit, that his questioning and the testimony he gave the Justices could not incriminate her in any way.

On the morning of the 19 July, Phoebe was clearing the dishes from breakfast and Phillis was out back tending to the wash, when Master Codman entered the kitchen, "Phoebe, prepare yourself, you are wanted at the Court for questioning. I will be escorting you there myself."

He noted her eyes widen, and her mouth gape open as if to ask a question, but she seemed to think better of it and remained silent, except for the mumbled, "Yes, sir."

She tried with all her might to hide her fear as they approached the Court. It was no use, try as she might, she could not conjure Quaco's encouraging words, nor Mark's promises of a better life.

She entered with Codman, sure that her guilt was evident to all she passed. Justice Stoddard waited patiently, looking intently at the latest witness in the Codman murder investigation. He could not have imagined what was about to happen.

Phoebe knew she was not innocent in the poisoning of Cap'n Codman, but rather a prime player in the drama which had unfolded so shortly before. Her mind was filled with confusion, should she confess and beg the mercy of the magistrate before her as she sold out her co-conspirators or should she lie and hope they did to? Would Mark, Phillis, and Robin protect her if she protected them? Could they all get away with murder if they stuck together? Or would they each try to save themselves?

Justice Stoddard's voice broke into her thoughts, "Was Captain John Codman, late of Charlestown, your master?"

Startled at his voice, her reply was louder than intended, "Yes, sir!" She realized too late it sounded like a shout.

"How long were you his servant?"

"For as long as I can remember, sir, and until his death, now his heir is my master, sir."

Stoddard continued, "Do you know the cause of your master's death?"

"I was told he was poisoned."

"Do you know if he was poisoned?"

"Sir, if I know something about it and I tell you what I know, can you help me?"

"What do you mean, Phoebe? Do you know something about your master's death? What kind of help do you want?"

"I don't want to die, sir," was the simple answer that escaped her lips, though not what she expected to say. It was too late now, it was out, he had heard it loud and clear.

"Well, now, I guess that depends on what you know and if it what you tell me is true. Would you like to tell me true and I'll see what I can do so that justice is served?" The justice smiled kindly as he spoke making Phoebe wonder if she could trust him or not.

"I believe I do, your honor, if you can help me?" She questioned still unsure if he was making any promises to her.

"Very well. Let's proceed. Do you know he was poisoned?

"Yes, sir, I do," she spoke softly and hesitantly. Thus, began her betrayal of her friends.

"What was he poisoned with?"

"It was a white powder, supposed to kill a man quickly with no traces. Also with the potter's lead, sir."

"How was he poisoned?" Justice Stoddard continued, disbelieving the truth could come so quickly and easily from her lips.

"Well, sirs, Mark Codman, got the white poison from Robin, Doc Clark's Negro. It didn't seem to be working the

147

way Robin told him it would, so then he got potter's lead from Essex, Power's Negro, as a back up to make sure the Captain died."

"So Mark poisoned the Captain?"

"Well, no sir. It wasn't quite like that, you see, this is where I need your help. Mark told his wife, Phillis, that since she was the house servant, she'd need to help him give the poison to the Cap'n when he took his meals. Then sir, Phillis told Mark, that they'd need to let me in on it, since I was always in the kitchen preparing the food with her."

"So, Phillis poisoned the Cap'n at the instruction of her husband? And you knew about it, but didn't tell anyone until now?"

"Not quite. Mark gave us both a pretty speech about how we could poison the Cap'n together and then we'd get a kinder master or maybe even be free. It sounded so good. He told me I could then get to see my husband, Quaco, more than one night a week, maybe even every day. That would've been a blessing to me. I wasn't quite convinced by what he said to tell you the truth. And my Quaco warned me to steer clear of Mark Codman's scheming. Quaco told me it would get me in a heap of trouble."

"Then Mark continued his pleading for our help, reminding us o' how the Cap'n had hurt ole Tom in a fit of rage and that we might be the next to feel his wrath. He even told us, along with Quaco, how we needed to do it for our betterment."

And if that wasn't enough to convince us, he told us the good book said it wasn't even murder if no blood was shed like in stabbing or cutting the Cap'n."

Stoddard continued, "So you helped Mark with his plan so you could be with your husband more often."

"Well, yes sir. I never had no family I can remember and I was hoping Quaco and I could maybe have one together. The promise of a better life is mighty strong, sir."

Ignoring her comment about a better life, Stoddard continued, "The point is that you did help Mark Codman with his plan. How did you carry it out?"

"Mark told us he'd bring the powder to us soon. He did, real soon, just a few days later. It was wrapped in paper, tied up, he gave it to me and Phillis, but he had lost the measuring tool, so he went to work in the blacksmith's shop to make a new one."

"So, when you got the measuring implement, what happened?"

"Well, he fixed it up and gave it to Phillis. She brought it to the kitchen and we mixed it up, by Mark's direction, with water in a vial and hid it in the kitchen closet behind a jug. We didn't intend to poison no one but the Cap'n, not the mistresses or master John or the others."

"Then how did you give just the Cap'n the poison and not the other family members?"

"Well, me and Phillis, we mixed it up in the Cap'n chocolate infusion, 'cause no one else took that drink."

"When was all this? Just before Captain Codman's death?"

Well, no sir, the Cap'n didn't go like we expected, though we used all the poison. Mark told us he'd get more and he did. It'd been nearly a week gone, and finally the Cap'n took sick. That day, when the mistresses asked for sago for their Pa, Phillis put in some more poison."

"You saw her do it?" Stoddard questioned.

"Yes, sir, then the next day, the mistresses again asked for sago for the Cap'n. That day Mark was in the kitchen with us, and he, himself put the potter's lead in it along with the white powder."

"Did he? He had then acquired more arsenic – the white powder – from Dr. Clark's Robin?" Stoddard glared, still shocked at how quick she was to give up her "friends" in an effort to save her own skin, as it were. Of course, she was admitting her own guilt as well and for that she would, as would the others have to be made an example for the good of the colony – to put down other such attempts at murder.

"Yes, sir, he did it sir. I didn't see him get more poison from Robin, sir, but that is who he said got it for him and he's not given to lying."

Stoddard had to subdue a chuckle, "not given to lying" she said, but okay with murder. Stoddard had never given much thought to the rights of slaves or the lack of rights, nor the life they lived before today. If he had to confess, he'd have said before hearing Phoebe that he thought they enjoyed the life they lived and were well-taken care of; but now, he wondered. Shaking his head and the thought away, that was a quandary to consider another day – today justice had to be served and punishment meted out quickly if murder had indeed been committed.

John Codman II, sat quietly, in shock, awed as he listened to the tale of his father's death unfold. *"How could Mark, beloved and trusted servant, act thusly?"* he thought as the anger rose within.

"Thank you, John, for bringing your servant in. I'd ask that you remain for a few moments as she is placed in the custody of the gaoler."

Phoebe gasped! *"What did he say? She was going to be imprisoned after all her help today?* She could scarcely believe what she was hearing.

Justice Stoddard addresses her briskly, "Phoebe, you will be held in the gaol for the time being, while we verify your story."

She knew better than to speak to the Justice in that way and remained silent, fearful of the look in master John's eyes. She was taken by a court official quickly to the gaol, where there would be plenty of time for her to ponder her fate.

Codman watched with fire in his eyes that was mellowed only by the tears which fell for his father's memory as he watched her taken away. He heard Justice Stoddard order two more officials to head to the Codman estate and bring Mark and Phoebe to the gaol. The charges would be determined and the trial, along with swift justice, would come quickly.

Chapter 9

The Trial

Phillis, doing the wash in the yard, had seen Phoebe head out early with Master John. She didn't know what to think at that time, but when she heard the knock on the door of the mansion, a feeling of dread overcame her. At that same moment, Mark stuck his head in the kitchen, totally unaware that Phoebe had gone to town with master John. Neither had time to speak, for the court officials arrived quickly in the kitchen.

Phillis and Mark were under arrest. Speaking to their Mistresses, they heard one of the officials declare, "They are to be questioned in the murder of your father, Captain John Codman."

It was the last time they would see the only home they had known for years. Panic overcame them, they were unable to speak, to protest, or to try to run.

26 July 1755

Within days, Phillis is before Justice Thaddeus Mason and Attorney General Edmund Trowbridge. She is quite simply terrified.

Justice Mason begins the query, "You were the servant of the Captain John Codman, late of Charlestown?"

Phillis, mustering her courage and knowing she must hold herself together, answers, "Yes, sir, I was."

"How long were you his servant?"

"From my childhood when he bought me all the way to his death."

"Do you know how he died?"

"I was told he was poisoned," she says simply.

Mason continues, "Do you know that he was poisoned?"

"Yes, sir. I know."

"What was he poisoned with?"

"It was with the potter's lead."

Trowbridge interrupts, "How do you know your master was poisoned with potter's lead?"

"Mark got the potter's lead from Essex, Powers' Negro. One of the mistresses found the lead in the porringer that held the Cap'n's sago. The Cap'n complained of a gritty taste and she found it after that. She asked me 'bout it, and I told her I didn't know what it was, but when I cleaned the skillet, I found some there, too. Then Tom found a paper in the blacksmith's shop and I knew it was the same lead that was in the porringer and the skillet."

"Do you know about any other poison that was given to Captain Codman?

"Yes, sir, it was in water poured out of a vial."

"How do you know that?" Trowbridge continues.

"The white powder in the vial of water could be seen 'cause it had sunk to the bottom."

"And do you know who put the powder in the vial?"

"Yes, sir, I did it first."

"Where did you get the powder?"

"Phoebe gave it to me in the garret where we sleep, on the Sabbath. She told me that Mark gave it to her."

"What was the powder in when you got it?"

"It was in white paper, folded in a square, tied with string."

Justice Mason proceeds, "How much powder was there?"

"A good amount, at least an ounce, I'd guess."

"Did you add all the powder to the vial?"

"No, sir, first I measured it with the tool Mark gave to me to give to Phoebe. I asked what it was and he wouldn't tell, but he did say that Robin gave him a tool like it and he lost it, so he made this one new in the blacksmith's shop. I gave it to Phoebe in the kitchen, then she gave it to me the next morning in the garret while Quaco was still there. She whispered to me to take the powder hidden by the window and put it in the vial, which I did. Then she told me to add water, which I didn't, but she did later. Phoebe then told me to hide it in the corner of the closet behind the black jug."

"Was your master served the water with the poison in it?"

"Yes."

"How was it given to him?"

"It was in his drink, his infusion, his chocolate, and his watergruel."

"Who put it there, in his food?" Justice Mason asked, shocked by the ease with which she told the story incriminating herself, her friend, and her husband.

"Phoebe did and then he ate it."

"Did she also put it in his beverage?"

"I did that myself. I poured it in, but then I felt dirty and poured it out. Then I put in fresh water.

Still amazed at the testimony being given, Mason continues, "Who poured the water into the infusion?"

"Phoebe did."

"How do you know?"

"I saw her do it." Phillis spoke hesitantly in hopes she would help herself by telling the truth. Though she was caught and terrified, she thought she might still save her own life, if only for the sake of caring for her remaining children.

"Did you see your master drink it?"

"Yes sir, a whole cup full of it."

"How do you know she poured the poison water into his chocolate?"

"She told me she did so, before he drank it, she said."

"Did you see him drink it?"

"Yes sir, he sat in the kitchen and ate it right there in front of us."

Trowbridge asks, "Who put the second powder into the vial?"

Phillis continues, "Phoebe did. I was in the cellar drawing cider, when I heard Phoebe tell Mark the powder was all used up."

"What day was this?"

"Wednesday before the Cap'n passed."

"Was any more powder obtained and given to your master?"

"Yes. Mark got it, but it wasn't ever given to the Cap'n."

"What did Mark do with it then?"

"He gave it me. It was white powder, same as the first."

"What was it in?"

"It was in the white paper, like the first, but this time Mark only gave me part of it, he tore the paper and kept the other half himself. He told me that Robin Clark said we should've given it to the Cap'n in two doses and it would've killed him and no one would have been the wiser. He said it would've been the same as how Mr. Salmon's Negros had poisoned him and got away with it. He said they got good masters and so would we."

Trowbridge fascinated queries, "What did you do with the white powder Mark gave you?"

A bit more relaxed, Phillis offers, "I put it in the same vial and hid it back in the closet."

"Was any of this water given to your master?"

"Not a drop, sir. He died the day after and Mark came to the kitchen just after, when I was having dinner, asking for the bottle. He took it and I never saw it again until Justice Mason showed it today."

The Justices look at one another momentarily, before continuing with the remainder of their questions. Both speculated, as Justice Stoddard had just a few days earlier, at the motivation of these slaves. The justices had never given much thought to the lives of their slaves before, nor any slaves for that matter. They were after all, merely property, here to serve their masters.

Phillis sits quietly waiting for the next questions to come. Perplexed, she wonders if they will ask her why they poisoned the Cap'n. They've asked already the how, what, and when questions, but never the why. They are freemen, the gentry, the men with all the rights who know nothing of the heartfelt need for freedom that tortures each and every slave – the unending desire for a better life, a free life, where families are not torn asunder at the whim of a master, where anger and absolute power are not the rulers of their lives. *How could they understand?*

Her thoughts are interrupted by Justice Mason, "Phillis, do you know where Mark got the poison powder?"

"He got it from Robin, Dr. Clark's Negro, the one who lives with Mr. Vassall from time to time."

"How do you know that?" Justice Mason continues with the questions.

"Well, sir, the Thursday before the Cap'n's death, Mark said he was going to Boston to get more powder from Robin. When he got back, I asked him if he got it and he says no, but Robin's bringing it on the morrow. The next night, a Negro fellow arrived asking for Mark, but he wouldn't tell me his name, even when I asked if he was Robin. He said he was from the country and had come to talk to Mark about his child. When I wouldn't call Mark, he left. I followed him as far as the ferry. Later on Mark told me if a Negro fellow came looking for him saying he was from the country with news about his child to come get him. I asked him what Negro and he told me it was Robin, but told me to tell no one about it."

"Do you know this Robin, Dr. Clark's Negro?"

"Yes I do and have for years."

"How then is it that you could not identify him the night he came?"

"It was too dark to see his face clearly, but I am certain it was Robin."

"How can you be sure?"

"That night, I told Mark about the Negro fellow who wanted to see him, he asked why I didn't call him. I told him I was called in by the mistress and could not. Mark said he was sad I did not. Then Mark asked if he left anything and I told him no. He said again, he was sorry he didn't and then I asked Mark who he was. He said Robin and that they had been playing Blind Man's Bluff going back over the ferry twice and missing one another. Finally, he went to Boston on Saturday, and returned with more powder on Monday.

"Did you see Robin at Charlestown near the time of your master's illness and death?"

"Yes, sir, I did. I saw him on Tuesday when the Cap'n's ship launched and the Cap'n caught Mark at Mrs. Sherman's buying a drink. I saw him on Saturday after the

Cap'n burial. I even told Phoebe on Tuesday when I saw him, I said there goes Robin. She asked me how I knew it was him and what he had on. I told her a black wig and a blue coat with yellow lining. I told Phoebe I thought he had gone up to tell Mark not to mention that he had given him anything and she thought so too. Later we went to the pump with a pail and he walked right by us looking me square in the eye and I knew it was Robin. Phoebe questioned if I was sure and I assured her I had known him for years and it was he.

Changing course a bit, Trowbridge asks, "Do you know what the white powder was?"

"Mark said it was Ratsbane, but I told Phoebe I thought he was lying, that it was burnt alum instead, because Ratsbane makes you swell and the master did not swell up at all."

"How many times was your master given the poison?"

"I believe it was seven."

"And to be clear, when was the first time?"

"The Monday after Phoebe gave it to me. Phoebe put it in his chocolate on Monday and then again on Wednesday, then again on Friday. I saw him drink it all three times. Then I put some in his watergruel on Saturday, but I felt ugly and threw it out. I made some more watergruel, poured it in and it turned yellow and was thrown out also. I don't believe he had more 'til Mark put in the potter's lead on Monday night."

"And how do you know Mark put the potter's lead into the sago?"

"I went out of the kitchen and when I came back Mark was there and afterward I found the lead in the skillet. Neither Phoebe nor I had any lead."

"Do you know of any other poison given your master?"

"No sir," Phillis answers, silently praying for this grueling session to be over.

It was not to be, as Trowbridge continued, "Who thought to poison your master?"

"Forgive me Mark," she thinks as she replies, "It was Mark, sir. He told us he had read the Bible through and it was no sin to kill him if no blood was shed in a violent manner – like stabbing or shooting him."

"When did Mark propose this poisoning?"

"Back in the winter at first, and Phoebe and I said no to such a thing. But then he came again proposing it about a fortnight ago. I said no, so he proposed it to Phoebe. He said he was uneasy for our safety, Phoebe and I, because of what happened to Tom and that he wanted a better master."

Changing the subject, Justice Mason asks, "Do you know how your master's work house burned down?

"Why you askin' about that? That were a long time past and don't have anything to do with this!" This line of questioning threw her even more. *How did they know about that fire?*

"Well," the justice answered slowly, "there might be a pattern here of the Cap'n's slaves trying to bring him harm. Is that what is happening here?"

"No sir."

Really? Let me ask the question again, just to be sure you understand, do you know how your master's work house burned down?"

Phillis looked defeated, and once again she resigned herself to tell the truth, "Yes, sir, I know what happened to the work house." She paused and then continued, "I set it on fire, because Mark wouldn't let me rest 'til I did it. Mark put the shavings down and I threw on a hot coal and left before the fire started."

"Did anyone else know?"

"Yes, Phoebe did. But she and Mark were already abed when I threw the coal on."

"Who thought to do it?"

"Mark did, thinking the master would sell us to cover the loss."

One more question, "When you found out about the poisoning plan, why did you not tell your Master or some of the family, and prevent it?"

Phillis, resigned to the truth, wearily replies, "I do not know, sir."

"That is all," were the words she heard as the gaoler removed her from the examination and set her back into her cell in the gaol. At first, she tried calling out to Mark, but no reply came. She knew they must be held separately probably at least until they were examined.

All she could think of now was how she had betrayed her beloved husband in hopes of remaining alive. And yet, what kind of life would she have without him? They had thrown what little happiness they had together away – for the dream of a better life, greater happiness, and freedom. She curled into a ball in the corner and cried unashamedly until exhaustion overwhelmed her.

Mark, in his own cell, called out for his wife well into the night, wanting to hear her voice, to comfort her in some small way; but silence was the only answer he heard. *"What is happening? What have we done?"*

27 July 1755

The following day, Mark finds himself in the seat so recently vacated by Phillis in the examination room. He, too, sits before Justice Thaddeus Mason and Attorney General Edmund Trowbridge.

Mason begins, "State your name."

"Mark Codman, sir."

"Are you a servant or a freeman?"

"I am a servant, currently of John Codman II, formerly of his father, Captain John Codman."

"How long were you his servant?"

"For several years, until his death." Mark felt an unexpected twinge of sadness, or maybe it was guilt, even as he spoke the words.

Mason notes the small, but evident reaction, and continues, "Do you know what caused your master's death?"

"He was poisoned."

"With what?"

Mark resigned himself to the truth as he saw it, even as his mind cried out to his wife for her forgiveness, "with poison that came from the Doc."

"What Doctor?"

"Doc Clark, the one who lives in the North End, sir, in Boston."

"What poison was it?"

"It was a white powder wrapped in paper and tied with twine."

Trowbridge, angered by the seeming calm of the witness, interjects, "How do you know the powder came from Doctor Clark's?"

"Robin, the Doc's Negro, gave it to me."

"When and where?"

"It was on a weekday night, at the Doc's barn."

"Was there anyone else with you?"

As he betrayed Robin, Mark recalled with fondness the support given him by Robin the entire time he had known him, "No sir."

"How many times did Robin give you the powder?"

"Only twice."

"When was the last time?"

"It was on the Sabbath, the day before the Cap'n died."

To corroborate his tale with Phillis and Phoebe's testimony, Justice Mason continues to press for details, "Where was it? What was it in?"

"We met again at his master's barn. The powder was wrapped in white paper, then brown paper on the outside."

"Why did he give you the powder?"

"It was to kill three pigs what belonged to Quaco, as Phoebe said," surprised at how easily the lie rolled off his tongue.

"How long ago since Robin gave you the first powder?"

"I can't recall."

"Was it before you and Robin met together at the Potter's workhouse?"

"I think it was, sir. About a week before that."

"Did you pay Robin?"

"No sir."

"What did you do with the powder?"

"The first I gave to Phoebe in the garret the night I got it; and she sent Phillis for the second, which I gave to her."

"What did Phoebe do with it?"

"She set in on the table."

"Did you give her all of it?"

"Yes, I gave it all to her just like Robin gave it to me."

"Did you tell her what was in it?"

"Well, no, she knew what it was, she is the one who told me what to get."

"What did she tell you to get?"

"Phoebe said to get something to kill three pigs."

"Did Robin tell you how to use it and what it would do?"

Mark continued in his lie, "He told me to put it in two quarts o' Swill and it would make the pigs swell up. I told Phoebe exactly what Robin told me on how to use it."

"Do you know if she used it?"

"No sir, except what she and Phillis told me since the Cap'n's death."

"And you gave the second powder to Phillis?"

"Yes sir to Phillis."

"When and where was that?"

"In the little house, the Monday before the master died."

"Did you give her all of it?"

"Yes sir. I took off the brown paper and gave it to her in the white wrapping. Then she carried it to the house and gave it to Phoebe just like Phoebe asked her to do."

"How then was your master poisoned with these powders?"

"Phoebe and Phillis told me they poisoned him with the powder."

"When did they tell you this?"

"They confessed it to me the day after he died."

"Were they together when they confessed to you?"

"No, sir. Phillis told me first, saying that Phoebe had used all the first powder that way, and that the two of them used the second that way. So, I went to Phoebe and asked her about it, and she says no at first, she didn't have anything to do with it. But then I told her what Phillis said to me, she owned it herself."

Justice Mason, listens, astonished at the ease of the lies, seeing now Mark is determined to save himself at any cost. Looking Mark straight in the eye, he continues the questioning, "So you didn't know they were planning to poison Captain Codman?"

Mark, notes the stare, but continues in his lie, "I did not. I had no reason to at all until I heard them on Saturday night before the Cap'n died discussing whether they had given him enough. What I did not know, nor who they were speaking of."

Mason presses, "So there was no discourse between you, Phoebe, and Phillis about the poison or getting more?"

"Phoebe told me on Friday, she had lost the powder and asked if I would get more from Robin for her, which I did. I picked it up from Robin on the Sabbath. When I returned, I gave it to Phillis to give to Phoebe."

"Was anyone with you? Did anyone see you and Robin together?" Justice Mason continued to press knowing the two had been seen multiple times together.

Mark, not knowing what the others had testified, continued his tale, "No, nobody else was there and I don't know that anyone saw us together."

"How long were you and Robin at the Potter's house?"

"Not long, I left Robin there, but he and the fellow with him followed me to the wharf, to Mrs. Sherman's, where I bought a toddy and shared it with them."

"Where did you all go after drinking the toddy?"

"They went to the ferry and I went to my masters with the pots I brought from the Potter's."

"Did either you or Robin exchange anything betwixt one another?"

"No sir."

"Did you call him back for anything?"
"No, sir."

"Did your master forbid Mrs. Sherman from selling you any more drink that day or any other?

Mark's eyes widen with wonder, "Yes, sir, he did," *wondering how the justices know this fact.*

"Did Robin know that happened?"

"Not that I know of, but Robin did see the Cap'n going to Mrs. Sherman's and told me," Mark realizing they knew all about this incident opted for the truth.

"Did you ever ask anyone else for poison?"

"Only Kerr, Doc Gibbon's Negro, 'cause Phoebe sent me to him. She'd asked him for it and he didn't give her any, saying he wanted to talk to Quaco first about the pigs. He didn't give it to me either, said he didn't have none."

"Did you ask Cato, Dr. Rand's Negro, for poison?

"No, I never did."

"Did you and Phoebe speak about your master in or around the mansion before your master died?

"Not that I know of."

"Did you say to Tom or any of the other of your master's servants that you knew the master would die soon?"

Mark notices the questions are coming faster and with more intensity, "No I did not, but the day before the Cap'n died, Phoebe came into the Blacksmith's shop to dress Tom's eye, where the Cap'n had hit him, and she was dancing about mocking the Cap'n's illness. Tom said he did not care if he never got up again on account of his eye. Scipio was there and he heard and saw it too."

Allowing Mark to continue his tales, Trowbridge continues, "Did you ever say that your master had been offered £400 for you but wouldn't take it?"

"I never said that."

Now, it was time to get down to the facts they had, Trowbridge queries, "Did you ever tell Phillis or Phoebe about a game of Blind Man's Bluff that you and Robin played at on the ferry when trying to meet one another, but rather instead, kept missing one another and that Robin was in disguise pretending to be a country Negro with word for you about your child?"

"I never told either of them anything like that," the lies came easier now, but he still marvels at where they got all their stories as he ponders Phillis, Phoebe, and Robin selling him out.

"How did the vial come to be buried near the blacksmith's shop on the Codman estate?

"I buried it."

"When?"

"The afternoon the master died."

"Where did you get it?"

"I took it from Phillis."

"Did anybody see you take it from her?"

"No, I took it from her after she told me she and Phoebe had used the poison on the Cap'n. When they confessed it to me, Phoebe begged me to say nothing about it. I told her if I'd known what she intended, I would never have got it for her. I had the vial in my pocket, and went to bury it but called Pompey down to the shop to show him, but before I could Mr. Kettell came to collect me and brought me here."

Justice Mason nods at the bit of truth in the last statement and carries on in another direction, "Have you had any potter's lead lately in your possession?"

Mark is weary, but continues, "Yes, what I got from Essex, Mr. Powers' Negro, which I got on the day I brought the pots home."

"What did you plan to do with it?"

"I was hoping to settle a score with Tom. Tom said it would melt in our fire, I said it wouldn't. I laid it up on a wall plate in the blacksmith's shop and never thought another thing about it 'til you showed it to me here."

"So, do you know if any of that lead or some like it was given to your master in his food or drink?"

"I do not," Mark replies trying to sound sure and true.

"Do you know of any proposal made to poison your master?"

"No, I do not, I never heard of any such thing."

"Do you know of any cashew nuts, copperas, or green stuff being provided for that purpose?"

"No, sir. I ain't seen no cashews since I been here in this country, not that others either."

"After you heard Phillis and Phoebe talking about giving him enough, why did you procure more poison for Phoebe?"

"I didn't know what they meant by what they were saying."

"Do you know anything more about your master's poisoning than you have told the court?"

"No, I do not."

"Mr. Kettle, please escort Mark Codman back to the gaol. There is no need for further isolation, we have the information we need."

The Bill of Indictment arrived in short order

following the witness examinations, the Justices deliberation,

and the evidence gathered. The jurors testified upon their

oath, Phillis, the Negro woman, servant of the late John

Codman, without the fear of God but with malice and

forethought, contrived to deprive her master of his life,

feloniously and traitorously, set out to kill and murder him.

On 13 June, in Charlestown, the said Phillis put the deadly

poison known as arsenic, maliciously, willfully, feloniously,

and traitorously in to a vial of water, and proceeded to poison

the watergruel of her master John Codman with it so that he

would be killed and murdered. Elizabeth Codman, daughter

of the late John Codman, did in all innocence, without

knowledge of the poison, give it to her father to eat. Said

John Codman, altogether ignorant of the plot and the poison

did then eat. He then languished for 15 hours and then died of poison. The said Phillis acted with malice forethought to willfully, feloniously, and traitorously kill and murder her master John Codman acting against the Peace of the Lord the King his Crown and Dignity.

Further, the Jurors upon their oath, testified, Mark, a Negro man, laborer, and servant of John Codman, and Robin, a Negro man, laborer and servant of William Clark, apothecary, in conjunction with the murder committed by Phillis, feloniously and traitorously advised, incited, and abetted the said Phillis to commit treason and murder against the Peace of the Lord the King his Crown and Dignity.

The Indictment was signed by Edmund Trowbridge, Attorney General and submitted by Caleb Dana, foreman.

The case was tried before Stephen Sewall, Chief Justice, along with Benjamin Lynde, John Cushing, and Chambers Russell, Associate Justices, each and every one well-read in the law. The clerks of court, jointly were Samuel

Winthrop and Nathaniel Hatch.

Chapter 10

The Verdict

Mark and Phillis were convicted. Though both pleaded not guilty, and for their trial put themselves upon God and Country, a jury including Foreman John Miller and 11 other good and lawful men of colony heard the evidence and returned guilty verdicts. The King's Attorney moved that Court bring the Judgement of Death against them both. Chief Justice Sewall on behalf of the Court pronounced the sentence of death in strict conformity to the common law of England.

The trial had spurred a great deal of discussion among the justices regarding slavery, slaves' rights or the lack thereof, and though they had not asked the slaves on trial why they had committed their crime – deep inside they knew. The justices marveled at how the motivation for freedom pushed these slaves to kill their master with no true guarantee of freedom – only the hope of it.

As Englishmen, was freedom such a strong motivator as it was for these slaves? Or was it something the English took for granted as freemen? Was slavery something freeman and slaves knew deep down was wrong and yet they suppressed the notion because it was the way of life in mother England and her colonies? Or was it something akin to greed for the English, because slaves meant wealth and status in the colonies and abroad?

English still, and yet American as well, which many had begun to consider themselves, they were feeling the pressures of taxation from their sovereign King George II and the control of the long arm of Parliament. As Americans, would freedom be a such a strong motivator – sooner rather than later – they would discover the answer.

And yet the justices knew what they had to do regardless of their questions about the right and wrong of slavery – their job was to uphold the law and in this case the law said that these slaves had no rights to rebel against their master. They had no right to retaliate against cruel behavior at the hands of their master, regardless of whether their children were sold or given away, regardless of whether they were beaten and maimed, regardless of how they were treated, they were merely property, like horses or cattle and were at the mercy of their master's absolute power.

Mark and Phillis Codman had obviously hoped for a better life – but instead, they would be an example for the slaves in the Massachusetts Bay Colony and beyond – a message to slaves everywhere. Their punishment would be a spectacle for all to see – swift and severe – intended to maintain order among the growing slave population in the colonies.

On 6 September, the warrant for the execution of Mark and Phillis is issued, under the official seal of the court, giving the command to Richard Foster, the Sheriff of

Middlesex, to carry out the last office of the law. The court ordered Phillis to be burnt to death and that Mark be drawn and hanged by the neck until dead with the admonition that God have mercy on their souls.

The execution is set for Thursday, 18 September 1755, to be carried out between the hours of one and five o'clock. This delay was in keeping with tradition and allowing time for the gallows to be constructed.

Chapter 11

The Wait

During the jury deliberation, all Mark, Phillis, and Phoebe could do was wait in desperation in their cells. Mark and Phillis understood the charge of Petit Treason, realizing it was rarely used but carried a wider berth than lesser charges that could have been filed against them. Petit Treason was the charge leveled against perpetrators in only three cases, more severe than 'simple' murder – first, in the case of a servant who killed his or her master or mistress, second in the case in which a wife killed her husband, and third in cases in which a clergyman killed his prelate or superior.

In the first case, if the servant were female, she would be burned at the stake; if the servant were a man, he would be drawn and hanged. To lessen the suffering of the guilty, the executioner fastened a cord to the stake and pulled it once the fire was set, holding it until death came. Often the cord burned through before death causing intense suffering from the flames.

In the case of hanging, the convicted felon was drawn to the place of execution on a sledge along the ground behind a horse. After the hanging, the body was often cut down, eviscerated, beheaded, quartered and disposed of as ordered. In other cases, typically by order of the sheriff presiding over the execution, the felon's body was instead taken from the gallows, gibbetted, that is hung in chains, often near the scene of the crime as a warning to all; until the elements or birds of prey disposed of it.

These were the thoughts plaguing the minds of Mark and Phillis as they waited. They also knew that the judge would soon set the note with the verdict and punishment into the hands of the sheriff to be carried out.

They did not have long to wait for the guilty verdict came quickly and with it the pronouncement of death. The thoughts which plagued their minds were coming to fruition.

Phoebe, her fate still unknown, heard the pronouncement as well and wondered, *"Would Justice Stoddard, help her as he had seemed to indicate, or was it a ruse to get her to confess her own guilt and testify against her friends?"*

She knew ultimately, and by her own admission, she had administered the bulk of the poison to the Cap'n. What was she to do, she wanted a better life, wanted to see her husband more than once a week, wanted to build a family with him, and most of all wanted to be free.

Freedom, it was the dream they had all shared. It was a dream they would not see on this earth, in this life. They had risked it all, taking a man's life in the process, and for Mark and Phillis, their freedom would come only in death, only by the mercy of God himself. For Phoebe, she knew not what fate awaited her and in her mind that was more terrifying than the future awaiting Mark and Phillis.

Chapter 12

The Punishment

The murder plot had been carried out in July of the year 1755. Captain John Codman, age 57, family man, master of slaves, was dead. His family mourned his death, his slaves did not. The murder by poison had been perpetrated by Mark, Phillis, and Phoebe Codman, slaves, property of Captain Codman.

They had been apprehended almost immediately as witnesses came forward. The investigation, followed by the trial, took two months to carry out justice, conveniently in exactly the amount of time required to construct the gallows.

September 17, 1755, was still shrouded in darkness when Mark found himself dragged from his cell, still shackled, his Parade of Death beginning as he was forced to follow slowly behind the minister and the magistrates toward the horse that would draw him to the gallows prepared especially for this event.

Terror filled his eyes, and he wondered in horror, yet again, was the freedom he sought worthy of the price he was about to pay? He cried out for mercy as he was prodded onto the sled-like rail, harnessed, and then drawn by the horse and rider to his own death. Would his freedom finally come in the midst of his release from this miserable life in which he found himself a prisoner, a slave, humiliated, the property of another man?

Even as death knell neared, Mark thoughts were overwhelmed at the sight of his dear wife, Phillis. How he loved her and now her blood would be on his hands. She had only sought to love him and aid him in the quest for freedom. Now for the love of him, she would also be executed mercilessly. He was overwhelmed with remorse, but there was no one he could unburden himself to, he would bare his guilt for eternity.

As his mind pondered his actions, he was sorely saddened at the thought of Phillis, alone, frightened, and now, soon to be executed, as he would be. And their children, soon to be without parents, and likely separated at the hands of the Codman heirs. He hoped when they were old enough they would understand his motivation – freedom – and against all odds, he hoped they would one day know the taste of freedom he had once known.

Mark's mind was diverted from his wife and children by the clamoring of the crowds. News of the execution had spread quickly throughout the countryside the day after the trial ended and the sentencing was announced. The news would be carried in the local newspapers, but word of mouth proved a much faster communicator for news such as this, particularly in so large a community.

Boston, was, after all, the largest of the colonial cities, boasting a population of 12,000 which included hundreds of black slaves, a lesser amount of Indian slaves and nearly 2,000 indentured white servants who would likely never earn their freedom. Three thousand, a fourth of the city's population, had gathered for the Parade of Death of Mark and Phillis Codman. The sentences would be carried out on the freshly constructed gallows at Charlestown Common. It was the largest gathering ever held in the city.

The Massachusetts Colony's laws were fashioned after British Law and the sentence of Petit Treason called for drawing – and Mark was feeling every step, every draw, as the rider pulled him to the gallows. It was ritual whose purpose was not lost on those in the crowd. Not only did drawing prolong the execution, but it served to maximize the effects of the message that punishment was inevitable for sinners, and death was the unescapable consequence for murder.

In spite of the message, the three thousand who gathered to watch the parade winding through the streets of Boston was almost festive. Almost. Mark could see the accumulation of emotions in their eyes – horror, anguish,

sympathy, sadness, hatred, anticipation, revenge, fear, anger –
there was no limit to the passions flowing forth as the Parade
of Death passed.

Some were horrified at the brutality of the executions
to come. They felt taking a life should be left to God. All men
(and women) would have to answer to God for their own
sins – Codman for his ownership of fellow human beings and
the slaves for their murder of him. Wasn't the spectacle they
were all about to witness – torture and execution – carried
out by the judgment of mere men? Did God truly condone
slavery, torture, and capital punishment or was it as Jesus
preached – "let him who is without sin cast the first stone?"

Others wondered at the institution of slavery and the
murder of John Codman. Was the poisoning caused in part
by cruelty or in full by slavery? Can one man ever have the
right to own others? Could slavery be justified or were those
held as slaves within their rights to seek any manner of

escape? Didn't the golden rule essentially speak against slavery?

Slaves were aghast as two of their own, oppressed souls like themselves, were led to the place of execution. The slaves were not there of their own accord, but forced to watch by their masters who hoped what they witnessed would prevent rebellion of their own slaves. They understood the execution of Mark and Phillis was meant as a lesson to them – this type of behavior would not be broached. The message clear – and not lost on them - freedom was not something to be sought, and yet how they longed for it. They appreciated what Mark had attempted, the goal of freedom at any cost, though many were appalled that he had actually carried out his plan.

Others in the crowd were excited. It was time for revenge, time to put slaves and servants in their place, to help them understand their position in society. After all, as slaveholders, they provided for their slaves – food, shelter, healthcare – allowing them to be free from the ills of poverty.

Many slave owners truly thought they were helping the slaves – who were believed to be biologically inferior to their masters.

The surviving Codman men were there, as well. Still outraged at their father's fate and at the hands of trusted slaves. Slaves who made their home alongside the family, but as property, nothing more. Dr. Clark was there as a friend of the family, still disbelieving what had occurred as well as the fact that his own slave Robin had been an accomplice to the crime, serving up the murder weapon from the doctor's own apothecary. Each of the men was deep in their own thoughts, looking on, as the parade concluded near the gallows, each knowing that justice would soon be served, and order restored to their community.

Also in the audience were the Clergy and the Colonial Officials bent on capitalizing on the opportunity before them to emphasize the need for moral living, as well as social order in the great city of Boston. They had worked for hours on end, preparing their speeches and sermons to be delivered as the accused stood on the gallows, convicted, shamed, and terrified, in tears and pleading for mercy. Mercy that would not come today, mercy that was preached from these same clergymen on any given church day.

Finally, among those in attendance were the accused. Forced again to confession, renouncing the Satanic influence which had inclined them to sin, ending their impassioned confession with heart-wrenching pleas for mercy and their lives.

Mark, again, felt the jerk of the drawing rail as the horse and rider made the turn into Charlestown Commons as the sun was rising ever so slowly in the eastern sky. At his first glimpse of the gallows, he wondered if he would expire from the sheer horror of what was about to transpire. He searched the crowd for his beloved Phillis, but his view was obstructed by his executioners, who roughly removed him from the rail and pushed him up the gallows stairs.

Suddenly the stench of molten tar, being prepared for him, scorched his nostrils. He felt as if his heart might stop, but it continued to drone on in its steady beating. In this surreal moment, he heard voices reading from the Bible "And thine eye shall not pity; but life shall go for life, eye for eye, tooth for tooth, hand for hand, foot for foot." The drawing had left him exhausted and confused, but the words rang true – he had read them himself.

Next, a new voice rang out with his name – Mark Codman, the crime – Petit Treason, followed by the penalty whose imposition had only begun, draw, hang, tar, gibbet. Hadn't he been through enough – brutally torn from his home and family, taken aboard ship, imprisoned in chains, hauled to the Americas, sold like an animal, and then cruelly mistreated at the hands of his master? He asked himself, what man, or woman, would not try to escape, to gain freedom, at whatever the cost?

He was jolted back to the present, as he was forced upright and the noose was placed about his neck. Just as the hood was lowered, he caught Phillis' eyes, wide with terror, wet with tears, awaiting her own fate, and yet tortured as she helplessly watched her much loved husband be tortured and killed. To his eternal dismay, he could do nothing to comfort her and at the same time, he could not stop himself from mouthing the words, "I'm sorry. I love you."

The black hood came down. He closed his eyes, resigned to his fate. There was nothing more that could be done, or could be said, he could only hope that the Savior, Jesus, about whom he had read in that Bible, truly forgave and saved the persecuted and the sinners leaving this world. He heard the click, the trap-door opening, and suddenly he was overcome with panic and fear, that faded as quickly as it had come into unconsciousness.

Phillis collapsed as Mark fell through the trap door. It was as if she lost all control of her faculties, she wanted to stay strong for Mark, but she could simply bear it no more. Her guards promptly resurrected her, and she went down again as the tarring began. Could they show no mercy?

Mark regained a bit of his faculties as the boiling pine tar was painted roughly against his skin and the odor of burning flesh reached his nostrils. He thought he heard the gathered crowd gasp collectively as he cried out in pain, again beseeching his torturers for mercy. But mercy would not be his that day. The only mercy he was afforded was not as a result of his cries – but at the whim of the Boston officials who believed themselves more humane than their British equivalents – and thus he would not be castrated and cut open to bleed out, an even more horrible fate. The tarring was merely another device intended to prolong the public display and the deliver the message – morality is the order of Boston and evil will be punished.

Mark could feel the lifeblood flowing from him as the torment took its toll on his already debilitated body and the gibbet clanged into place on Charlestown Common. Though the guards prodded and poked, Mark could not bring his body to move, so they hoisted him roughly into the iron gibbet. To Mark, in his current state, it was merely the exchange from one cage to the next – slavery to prison to the gibbet – death appeared to be the only true release.

Reconciled to death, Mark closed his eyes and breathed deeply as he was winched into position and awaited the Angel of Death.

It was as if Phillis could feel Mark will her to quietness. She allowed herself to be led demurely up the gallows stairs. Though she feared what was to come, something in her spirit kept her silent though her heart cried out in terror. She listened as her name was stated – Phillis Codman, slave, property of Captain John Codman, wife of slave Mark Codman, convicted of Petit Treason, sentenced to death – to hang until delirium set in and then to burn alive.

How could this be happening? How could the dreams she and Mark had for a better life end here at the gallows?

She saw the crowd through tear-filled eyes and her Mark, still and silent, in the gibbet cage, unrecognizable. Phillis felt the noose placed 'round her neck and watched with eerie calm as the executioner placed the other end of the rope on the burn stake. Though she had been forced to watch executions of this kind before, she pushed the reality out of her mind and thought of Mark and the life they'd hoped for – a life of freedom. She felt the noose tighten and cut off her breath, delusion set in, though she could still smell the tar boiling, that same tar so recently applied to her husband Mark.

The audience, some quiet, others sobbing, and yet others still calling for her death, seemed to grow distant as she fell into a state of semi-consciousness. She smelled the flames and felt the heat as the flames of the stake burned higher. She let out one final chilling scream as the flames began to engulf her and she experienced pain beyond imagination. The horrified scream startled the citizenry who had been stupefied by her silence.

A communal gasp was the last thing she heard, as the executioner released the cord and gifted Phillis with the ultimate relief from the flames. Mark had regained consciousness for one single moment when he heard Phillis' blood curdling cry as the flames began to tear away her skin. He felt her leave him in an instant as the crowd grew silent, the spectacle nearly at its end.

All the while, little thought had been given to Phoebe, their traitorous co-conspirator, who had turned on them to save her own life. And yet, there she stood, only a few feet away, in shackles, forced to watch the executions of those she had once called friends, those with whom she'd shared the dream of freedom. Phoebe was terrified, her fate yet unknown, but she wondered, could her destiny be even worse... after all, at least Mark and Phillis were now free.

Phoebe had little time to wait to discover her lot. Her guards left her no time to grieve for Mark and Phillis, and little time for remorse. The beating she had suffered at the hands of the prisoners and allowed by the guards had left her weak and weary and now the guards pulled her forward, dragging her head on into the future. Through the city they plodded, toward the docks she realized. What could be happening? What was her punishment to be?

The sentence was harsh, she thought, even more so than that of Mark and Phillis. At least, now in death they were free, but she had been sentenced to a lifetime of further torture in the heat of the Caribbean sugar plantations, where ruthless masters were more notorious than any slave owner in Boston.

Soon she found herself being forced aboard a ship bound for the Caribbean. The name of which, she knew not, for she could not read. The destination, she did not know. South and sugar, she heard the guards say. Her last thought as

211

she sat in irons among a numberless throng she did not know, headed for a port unknown – I am still a slave, sold again, separated once more from all that is familiar and all those I love…

Chapter 13

The Future

Though the news of the executions traveled quickly through Boston and the surrounding area, the only account carried by the news appeared in the Boston Evening Post on 22 September, 1755 and read thusly:

"Thursday last, in the afternoon, *Mark*, a Negro Man, and *Phillis*, a Negro Woman, both Servants to the late *Captain John Codman* of *Charlestow*n, were executed at *Cambridge*, for poisoning their said Master, as mentioned in this Paper some Weeks ago. The Fellow was hanged and the Woman burned at the Stake about Ten Yards distant from the Gallows. They both confessed themselves guilty of the

Crime for which they suffered, acknowledged the Justice of their Sentence, and died very penitent. After Execution, the Body of *Mark* was brought down to *Charlestown* Common, and hanged in Chains, on a Gibbet erected there for that purpose."

The only other account recorded regarding the events of the day was that of one Doctor Josiah Bartlett who states:

"The place where Mark was suspended in irons was on the northerly side of Cambridge Road, about one fourth of a mile above our Peninsula. The witness, Phoebe, who was the most culpable became powerful evidence against the other conspirators and escaped death, her punishment was her transportation to the West Indies, still enslaved."

*****

The case of Mark, Phillis, and Phoebe quickly faded from memory, except in the minds of those who witnessed the events and still remain. As time marches on, even the documentation of the case of Mark, Phillis, and Phoebe, including the execution warrant below, exists sparingly, save a few court documents, which support the facts reported and referenced in these events.

Middlesex, SS — September the 18th, 1755.

I Executed this warrant as above directed, by causing Phillis to be burnt to Death, and Mark to be hang'd by the neck until he was dead, between the hours of one and five a Clock of Said day —

Richd. Foster *Sheriff*

As the years fly forward, the colonists find new challenges facing them, struggles to maintain their own rights as British citizens, rights they feel the motherland of Great Britain and her Sovereign King George are continually in violation of, and thus stories of the slave struggles of those who came after Mark, Phillis, and Phoebe, were pushed out of view, if only momentarily, only to rear their heads again another day.

*****

AFTER YEARS

A few short years after the Codman incident in Boston, in 1758, the Pennsylvania Quakers act against the tyranny that is slavery, forbidding their members from owning slaves or participating in the slave trade. The act takes place during the global conflict known as The Seven Year's War. It goes relatively unnoticed in the British Colonies of America who are caught up in the French and Indian War, a part of the larger Seven Year's War.

At its end in 1763, the Seven Year's War left the motherland, Great Britain, in possession of greater territories in North America, but more significantly in a great deal of debt. In order to pay for the war, so recently waged, King George III and His Parliament decided to tax the American Colonies. In their minds, they saw the colonies growing rich as a result of the great victory won by the Empire as well as the fertile trading agreements with Great Britain.

The taxation began with taxes on printed documents and publications, and was followed by taxing colonial imports like tea and sugar.

The Massachusetts Bay Colony, and, in particular, Boston, was notably vocal, even to the point of hostility, regarding Parliament's policy.

The "Sons of Liberty" were born as a result of burgeoning anti-British sentiments and grew exponentially attracting members from all around the American Colonies.

In 1773, slaves living in Massachusetts, petition the government for their freedom. There efforts fail, even amid the colonists cries for freedom.

The same year, Phillis Wheatley, slave of the Wheatley family, becomes the first published African American poet when a London publisher releases *Poems on Various Subjects, Religious and Moral*, a collection of her verses.

With an ever-expanding population numbering 2.7 million in 13 colonies, the Continental Congress prepares to meet, as Connecticut, Rhode Island, and Georgia prohibit the importation of slaves to their colonies. Virginia in turn, also acts against slave importation.

In addition to the resistance to government oppression, the Continental Congress also addressed an issue at the heart of the early abolitionist movement – issuing a pledge to stop the importation of slaves to America. The anti-slavery movement had, of course, begun on the heels of the institution of slavery itself. In the American Colonies, the sentiment had been growing for years now, backed by a small, but growing number of loud, powerful voices.

No doubt, the members of the first Continental Congress had heard the voices. In Philadelphia where the Congress convened, voices loomed large in the words of Thomas Paine declaring, "That some desperate wretches should be willing to steal and enslave men by violence and murder for gain is rather lamentable than strange. But that many civilized, nay, Christianized people should approve, and be concerned in the savage practice, is surprising." If not

Paine's words, then possibly the words of Anthony Benezet, "Without purchasers...there would be no [slave] trade; and consequently, every purchaser as he encourages the trade, becomes partaker in the guilt of it."

The delegation from Virginia had likely heard the poignant voice of Patrick Henry, who on reading Benezet's writings, affirmed slavery, "repugnant to humanity... inconsistent with the Bible, and contrary to the principles of liberty."

Reverend Samuel Hopkins, speaking out against the immorality of slavery where his words led to the abolition of slavery in Rhode Island that same year.

The delegation from Massachusetts had heard the heart-wrenching plea from Prince Hall, a former slave now free, on behalf of those still held in bondage, "The petition of a great number of blacks detained in a state of slavery in the bowels of a free and Christian country humbly show that... they have in common with all other men: a natural and inalienable right to that freedom which the Great Parent of the Universe has bestowed equally on all mankind, and which they have never forfeited by any compact or agreement whatever.

They were unjustly dragged by the hand of cruel power from their dearest friends, some of them even torn from the embraces of their tender parents – from a populous, pleasant and plentiful country, in violation of laws of nature and of nations, and in defiance of all the tender feelings of humanity brought here to be sold like beasts of burden and like them condemned to slavery for life…

Every principle from which America has acted in the course of their unhappy difficulties with Great Britain pleads stronger than a thousand arguments in favour of [the anti-slavery] petitioners, and they, therefore humbly beseech that your honours give this petition its due weight and consideration and cause an act of the Legislature to be passed, whereby they may be restored to the enjoyments of that which is the natural right of all men; and their children, who were born in this land of liberty, not be held as slaves."

The abolition voices rose and fell in every colony, never silenced, but yearning for the freedom, rights, and equality that the members of the Continental Congress now found themselves calling for from King George and Parliament.

The resistance to the King's oppression and Parliament's declaration of Massachusetts's open rebellion only served to make things more difficult for General Gage and his troops. The residents of Massachusetts responded quickly, gathering up arms and organizing widespread militia units. Gage and his men had been given the royal order to use force against the colonies, beginning with the seizure of gunpowder stored up by the militia in Concord. They were given marching orders, as it were, for 19 April 1775.

Little did they know that Paul Revere, Charles Dawes, and Samuel Prescott had been sent to warn the militia at Concord that the British Regulars were set to march on them on the morrow.

18 April 1775

Dr. Warren has already sent Mr. Dawes ahead by land when Paul Revere arrives. The plan is laid for the signal in the North Church Steeple, if by water, two lanterns; if by land, one lantern. Paul Revere sets out from Charlestown, at the behest of Dr. Warren, to warn Hancock and Adams, who were believed to be Gage's target. Revere's thoughts are a jumble of what lies ahead, *"the night is dark and uncannily quiet. A multitude of thoughts spirit through my mind as I race to warn my friends and compatriots of the impending danger. Abruptly my deliberations are halted, as I pass an old, gibbeted skeleton hanging eerily in Charlestown. It is Mark, who has hung disturbingly here for many years now. My mind strangely recalls the murder accusations, the trial, and the punishment from*

20 years hence. I could still hear the voices, from all sides, shouting, some filled with reason and understanding, others outraged and seeking vengeance.

Was there a lesson to be learned from those dreadful events of 1755? Did one man have the right to own another and treat them as they saw fit? Was there another way? My thoughts drift away in the debate wondering what implications it would have should we truly break free from the oppression of King George and His Parliament? Did the slavery question all boil down to right or wrong or was the question and the answer even deeper still? Wasn't the freedom that Mark sought all those years ago, the very same freedom, we now desire from our oppressors, our Sovereign King George and Parliament?

The details sprang afresh in my mind as I recall Mark's arrest and those of his accused co-conspirators, Phillis and Phoebe. I remember their testimonies, the freedom they sought. Might we have to pay the ultimate price, like Mark and Phillis, to secure our freedom in the days ahead?

*****

The early abolitionists voices did not go completely unheeded, as Black Minutemen, came alongside colonists in the early battles of the Revolution in Lexington and Concord, Massachusetts.

Later that year General Washington banned the enlistment of free blacks and slaves in the growing colonial army. By years' end, he lifts the ban, ordering the Continental Army to accept the service of free black men.

Even the British joined in, with Virginia Governor John Murray, Lord Dunmore, offering any slave who fought on the side of the British their freedom following the War.

The war years following the 1776 Declaration of Independence by the Continental Congress, would see many changes come as the fledgling country emerged.

In 1777, Vermont led the way, becoming the first of the thirteen colonies to abolish slavery and enfranchise all adult males. New York followed suit, somewhat, enfranchising all free propertied men regardless of color or prior servitude.

It was, at least, a beginning.

Slavery Timeline

1501

Spanish settlers bring slaves from Africa to the Dominican Republic.

1522

Caribbean Slaves rebel.

1562

Britain joins Slave Trade.

1581

First slaves in Spanish Florida St. Augustine.

1619

First 20 slaves in Virginia.

1626

The Dutch imports 11 black slaves into New Netherlands.

1636

Colonial North America's slave trade begins when the first American slave carrier, Desire, is built and launched in Massachusetts.

1640

John Punch, a runaway black servant is the first documented slave for life.

1641

Massachusetts is the first colony to legalize slavery.

1643

The New England Confederation of Plymouth, Massachusetts, Connecticut, and New Haven adopts a fugitive slave law.

1650

Connecticut legalizes slavery.

1652

Rhode Island passes laws restricting slavery and forbidding enslavement for more than 10 years.

1652

Massachusetts requires all black and Indian servants to receive military training.

1654

A Virginia court grants blacks the right to hold slaves.

1660

Charles II, King of England, orders the Council of Foreign Plantations to devise strategies for converting slaves and servants to Christianity.

1662

Hereditary slavery Virginia law decrees that children of black mothers "shall be bond or free according to the condition of the mother."

Massachusetts reverses a ruling dating back to 1652, which allowed blacks to train in arms. New York, Connecticut, and New Hampshire pass similar laws.

In Gloucester County, Virginia the first documented slave rebellion in the colonies takes place.

1663

Maryland legalizes slavery.

1664
Maryland is the first colony to forbid interracial marriages.
New York and New Jersey legalize slavery.

New York, New Jersey, the Carolinas, Virginia, and Maryland
mandate lifelong servitude for all black slaves.

1676
In Virginia, black slaves and black and white indentured
servants participate in Bacon's Rebellion.

1680
The State of Virginia forbids blacks and slaves from bearing
arms, prohibits blacks from congregating in large numbers,
and mandates harsh punishment for slaves who assault
Christians or attempt escape.

1688
The Pennsylvania Quakers pass the first formal antislavery
resolution.

1691
Virginia passes the first anti-miscegenation law, forbidding
marriages between whites and blacks or whites and Native
Americans.

Virginia prohibits the manumission of slaves within its
borders.

South Carolina passes the first comprehensive slave codes.

1696
The Royal African Trade Company loses its monopoly and
New England colonists enter the slave trade.

1700

Pennsylvania legalizes slavery.

1702

New York passes Act for Regulating Slaves. Among the prohibitions of this act are meetings of more than three slaves, trading by slaves, and testimony by slaves in court.

1703

Massachusetts requires those masters who liberate slaves to provide a bond of 50 pounds or more in the event that the freedman becomes a public charge.

Connecticut assigns the punishment of whipping to any slaves who disturb the peace or assault whites.

Rhode Island makes it illegal for blacks and Indians to walk at night without passes.

1705

Slaves as property describing slaves as real estate, Virginia lawmakers allow owners to bequeath their slaves and to "kill and destroy" runaways.

Massachusetts makes marriage and sexual relations between blacks and whites illegal.

1711

Pennsylvania prohibits the importation of blacks and Indians.

1711

Rhode Island prohibits the clandestine importation of black and Indian slaves.

1712

Slave revolt: New York slaves in New York City kill whites during an uprising, and Nineteen rebels are executed.

1712

New York declares it illegal for blacks, Indians, and slaves to murder other blacks, Indians, and slaves.

1715

Rhode Island legalizes slavery.

1717

New York enacts a fugitive slave law.

1723

Virginia abolishes manumissions.

1732

Slaves aboard the ship of New Hampshire Captain John Major kill both captain and crew, seizing the vessel and its cargo.

1733

Quaker Elihu Coleman's "A Testimony against That Anti-Christian Practice of MAKING SLAVES OF MEN" is published.

1735

Louis XV, King of France, declares that when an enslaved woman gives birth to the child of a free man, neither mother nor child can be sold. Further, after a certain time, mother and child will be freed.

1738

Spanish Florida promises freedom and land to runaway slaves.

1739

Slaves in Stono, South Carolina rebel killing whites and seeking freedom in Florida, the revolt results in the deaths of 40 blacks.

1740
South Carolina passes the comprehensive Negro Act, making it illegal for slaves to move abroad, assemble in groups, raise food, earn money, and learn to read English. Owners are permitted to kill rebellious slaves if necessary.

Georgia and Carolina attempt to invade Florida in retaliation for the territory's policy toward runaways.

1749
Georgia repeals its prohibition and permits the importation of black slaves.

1751
George II repeals the 1705 act, making slaves real estate in Virginia.

1755
Three slaves kill their master John Codman and are hung, gibbeted, burned at the stake, and shipped into lifelong slavery in the Caribbean.

1758
Pennsylvania Quakers forbid their members from owning slaves or participating in the slave trade.

1770

Escaped slave, Crispus Attucks, is killed by British forces in Boston, Massachusetts. He is one of the first colonists to die in the war for independence.

1773

Slaves in Massachusetts unsuccessfully petition the government for their freedom.

Phillis Wheatley becomes the first published African-American poet when a London publishing company releases a collection of her verse.

1774

Connecticut, Rhode Island, and Georgia prohibit the importation of slaves.

Virginia takes action against slave importation.

1775

In April, the first battles of the Revolutionary war are waged between the British and Colonial armies at Lexington and Concord, Massachusetts. Black Minutemen participate in the fighting.

In July, George Washington announces a ban on the enlistment of free blacks and slaves in the colonial army. By the end of the year, he reverses the ban, ordering the Continental Army to accept the service of free blacks.

In November, Virginia Governor John Murray, Lord Dunmore, issues a proclamation announcing that any slave fighting on the side of the British will be liberated.

1776

In Philadelphia, Pennsylvania, members of the Continental Congress sign the Declaration of Independence.

1777

Vermont is the first of the thirteen colonies to abolish slavery and enfranchise all adult males.

New York enfranchises all free propertied men regardless of color or prior servitude.

1780
A freedom clause in the Massachusetts constitution is interpreted as an abolishment of slavery. Massachusetts enfranchises all men regardless of race.

1784
Abolition Effort Congress narrowly defeats Thomas Jefferson's proposal to ban slavery in new territories after 1800.

1790
First United States Census - Nearly 700,000 slaves live and toil in a nation of 3.9 million people.

1793
Fugitive Slave Act - The United States outlaws any efforts to impede the capture of runaway slaves.

1794
Cotton Gin - Eli Whitney patents his device for pulling seeds from cotton. The invention turns cotton into the cash crop of the American South—and creates a huge demand for slave labor.

1808
United States bans slave trade importing African slaves is outlawed, but smuggling continues.

1820

Missouri Compromise - Missouri is admitted to the Union as a slave state, Maine as a free state. Slavery is forbidden in any subsequent territories north of latitude.

1831

Slave Revolt - Virginia Slave preacher Nat Turner leads a two-day uprising against whites, killing about 60. Militiamen crush the revolt then spend two months searching for Turner, who is eventually caught and hanged. Enraged Southerners impose harsher restrictions on their slaves.

1835

Censorship - Southern states expel abolitionists and forbid the mailing of antislavery propaganda.

1847

Frederick Douglass's Newspaper - escaped slave Frederick Douglass begins publishing the North Star in Rochester, New York.

1849

Harriet Tubman escapes - After fleeing slavery, Tubman returns south at least 15 times to help rescue several hundred others.

1852

Uncle Tom's Cabin published - Harriet Beecher Stowe's novel about the horrors of slavery sells 300,000 copies within a year of publication.

1857

Dred Scott Decision - The United States Supreme Court decides, seven to two, that blacks can never be citizens and

that Congress has no authority to outlaw slavery in any
territory.

1860
Abraham Lincoln of Illinois becomes the first Republican to
win the United States Presidency.

Southern Secession - South Carolina secedes in December.
More states follow the next year.

1861-65
United States Civil War - Four years of brutal conflict claim
623,000 lives.

1863
Emancipation Proclamation - President Abraham Lincoln
decrees that all slaves in Rebel territory are free on January 1,
1863.

1865 Slavery Abolished - The 13th Amendment to the United
States Constitution outlaws slavery.

References

Alden, J. R. (1954). *The American Revolution, 1775-1783* (Vol. 10). In the Hands of a Child.

American Imprints Collection, Rare Book and Special Collections Division. (3-1).

Apidta, Tingba. (2003). Black Timeline of Massachusetts, *A History of White Supremacy in the Bay State.*

Benezet, A., & Society of Friends. London Yearly Meeting. (1760). *Observations on the Enslaving, importing and purchasing of Negroes.* Christopher Sower.

Blumrosen, A. W., & Blumrosen, R. G. (2006). *Slave Nation: How Slavery United the Colonies and Sparked the American Revolution.* Sourcebooks, Inc.

Carp, B. L. (2010). *Defiance of the Patriots.* Yale University Press.

Christian, Charles M. (1995). "Black Saga" *The African American Experience*, Houghton Mifflin Company.

Douglas, Frederick. (1845). *An American Slave*, District Court of Massachusetts.

Emerson, E. W. (2013). *The Complete Works of Ralph Waldo Emerson* (Vol. 11). Read Books Ltd.

Emerson, W. (1972). Diaries and Letters of William Emerson, 1743–1776.*Minister of the Church in Concord, Chaplain in the Revolutionary Army.*

Farrow, A., Lang, J., & Frank, J. (2006). *Complicity: How the North promoted, prolonged, and profited from slavery.* Random House Digital, Inc.

Fenn, Elizabeth. (2001). *"Pox Americana" The Great Smallpox Epidemic of 1775-1782.* Hill and Wang.

Fischer, D. H. (1995). *Paul Reveres Ride.* Oxford University Press.

Forbes, E. (1999). *Paul Revere and the world he lived in.* Houghton Mifflin Harcourt.

Gluster, Irwin &Ketchum, Richard M. (1971). *American Testament, Fifty Great Documents of American History.*

Goodell, A. C. (1883). *The Trial and Execution, for Petit Treason, of Mark and Phillis: Slaves of Capt. John Codman, who Murdered Their Master at Charlestown, Mass., in 1755; for which the Man was Hanged and Gibbeted, and the Woman was Burned to Death; Including, Also, Some Account of Other Punishments by Burning in Massachusetts* (Vol. 1755). J. Wilson and Son.

Greene, L. J. (1942). Negro in colonial New England, 1620-1776.

Hall, M. G., & Schutz, J. A. (1962). William Shirley: King's Governor of Massachusetts.

Hall, P., White, W., Holt, R., Forbes, B., Middleton, G., Mantone, P., ... & Hill, L. (1936). Documents Relating to Negro Masonry in America. *The Journal of Negro History, 21*(4), 411-432.

Henry, W. W. (1891). *Patrick Henry; life, correspondence and speeches* (Vol. 3). Charles Scribner's sons.

Jefferson, T., & Johnston, R. H. (1903). *The Writings of Thomas Jefferson* (Vol. 20). Issued under the auspices of the Thomas Jefferson memorial association of the United States.

Jennings, F. (1990). *Empire of Fortune: Crowns, Colonies, and Tribes in the Seven Years War in America*. WW Norton & Company.

Jordan, D., & Walsh, M. (2008). *White cargo: The forgotten history of Britain's white slaves in America*. NYU Press.

Lemire, E. (2011). *Black Walden: Slavery and Its Aftermath in Concord, Massachusetts*. University of Pennsylvania Press.

Life of Henry Wadsworth Longfellow with Extracts from his Journals and Correspondence. (1891). Three Volumes. Houghton Mifflin.

List of Tea Party Participants, 2016 Old South Meeting House, Boston Massachusetts.

Middlekauff, R., & Woodward, C. V. (1982). *The Glorious Cause: The American Revolution, 1763-1789* (Vol. 2005). New York: Oxford University Press.

Muraskin, W. A. (1975). *Middle-Class Blacks in a White Society: Prince Hall Freemasonry in America*. University of California Press.

Robertson, E. S., & Anderson, J. P. (1887). *Life of Henry Wadsworth Longfellow*. Associated Faculty Press Inc.

Schutz, J. A. (1961). *William Shirley, King's Governor of Massachusetts.* University of North Carolina Press.

Second Massachusetts Historical Collection. Vol. II, p. 166 and subsequent note.

Taylor, Dale. (1997). "Everyday Guide to Life in Colonial America from 1607 -1783" A Writers Guide. Writer's Digest Books.

Thoreau, Henry D. (2015). "Slavery in Massachusetts" Copyright African Free Press Pamphlet Series

Wesley, C. H. (1983). *Prince Hall, Life and Legacy.* United Supreme Council, Southern Jurisdiction, Prince Hall Affiliation.

Wheatley, P. (1887). *Poems on various subjects, religious and moral.* WH Lawrence.

Wood, G. A. (1920). *William Shirley, Governor of Massachusetts, 1741-1756: A History* (No. 209). Columbia University.

Wright, L. B., Commager, H. S., & Morris, R. B. (2002). *The cultural life of the American colonies.* Courier Corporation.

Vaver, A. (2011). *Bound with an iron chain: The untold story of how the British transported 50,000 convicts to colonial America.* Pickpocket Publishing.

Williams, John B. (April 2015). "The Grimshaw Offensive." The Phylaxis (magazine), The Phylaxis Society.

Made in the USA
Middletown, DE
02 December 2023